THIS BOOK IS F[

- You're a Headteacher or Senior Lead~. ~~~~~ proven to have more impact than anything else on EVERY asp~~ school improvement (and has no 'sell-by' date!)

- You're trying to eliminate poor quality teaching, staff inconsistency and underachievement so you can raise standards and stop dreading 'Results Day' or getting 'The Inspection Call'.

- You're a busy School Leader, Teacher or member of Support Staff and you'd like to take a 'Coach Approach' in your everyday work (with colleagues, pupils and parents) so that you can save time and stop feeling so drained, overwhelmed and under pressure.

- You want to stop 'spoon-feeding' the people you work with so they can become more engaged, more confident and more empowered – and make MUCH more progress!

- You're open to learning some simple, practical coaching strategies which will immediately make a dramatic difference in improving mental health and wellbeing, behaviour and grades.

- You'd rather do what's right for your children and what's guaranteed to get the best outcomes instead of wasting your time, energy and money on the latest government initiative or educational fad.

- You want to learn how coaching has changed dramatically over the years and why 'old hat' models (like GROW, TGROW, OUTCOMES, COACH, OSKAR, STRIDE and CEDAR) set off alarm bells and lack impact.

- You're a new or experienced coach in a school and you want to hone your core coaching skills, fast-track your success or find out how to work less hard and make much more impact in your coaching.

- You're in charge of coaching or writing coaching into your school improvement plan and you want tips, ideas and a logical strategy for developing and embedding coaching for maximum impact and sustainability.

- You want to be inspired by other schools who have achieved success with my coaching approach.

WHAT PEOPLE ARE SAYING ABOUT ANNIE'S WORK

"Annie's approach has revolutionised how we empower colleagues to make the difference in their classrooms. It's timely, targeted and most importantly the impact is felt across our school community. Not all coaching is the same. If you are thinking of investing in a coaching model then invest in this one – it works!"

Amanda Simpson, Headteacher, Tunbridge Wells Grammar School for Boys

"It has had a measurable impact on lesson grades and the quality of teaching & learning."

Russ Barr, Assistant Director, Schools and Learning, Derbyshire County Council

"It is rare to find CPD that has such an immediate impact. It has transformed the way senior and middle leaders feed back to colleagues after lesson observations and as part of the appraisal process. All too often CPD is aimed at a specific type of school - primary, secondary or special school. As a special school Head I can honestly say that *Coaching in Schools* is as relevant to our school as any other sector in education. Being coached has really helped me to prioritise and work effectively across two schools."

Debbie Foolkes, Headteacher, Woodlands Secondary School & Lady Zia Wernher School

"I have completed coaching training before but I prefer Annie's method because it is simple to use, easy to remember and the approach can have impact not only in improving the quality of teaching and learning, but it can also support the development of whole school appraisal processes, communication with children and increase the skills of the coach in self-evaluation and reflection."

Catriona Goldsmith, Headteacher, Palatine Primary School

"We have put well over 40 teachers and support staff through this training and use it with colleagues in partner schools because it works! The methodology of the training means that skills are built up over time and stick. The results are tangible and can be personalised so that both coaches and coachees are motivated to participate – and to come back for more. We have seen the impact in school in terms of classroom practice, leadership, time management and workload management. It is the backbone of our CPD programme."

Mary Davies, Executive Headteacher, Maiden Erlegh Trust

"As a Headteacher of a very busy secondary school I have found the techniques in the coaching programme have empowered my teams to empower others. The result is that staff have the time to reflect and solve their own problems, ensuring that they are learning how to lead and manage teams in an effective and efficient way."

Karen Johns, Headteacher, Stopsley High School

"The model and techniques are extremely practical and realistic for use in a school. The training has sharpened my approach and helped the school culture to develop further."

John Burridge, Headteacher, Lealands High School

"The coaching programme has made a significant contribution to school improvement."

Martin Reynolds, Headteacher, Brownedge St Mary's Catholic High School

"*Coaching in Schools* brings a straightforward approach to helping not only staff but also students, to move forward in their school lives. It gives them the ownership of problems and puts them at the centre of the decision-making process as they explore potential solutions and ideas. A coaching programme which values the person and through which the person feels valued!"

Chris Dean, Headteacher, Icknield High School

"Completing my *Coaching in Schools* online training has transformed my thinking and the way I speak to and listen to my colleagues in different contexts. The 'bite size' units are easy to digest and the modules are convenient to complete - even within busy school days! The tasks are all relevant, useful and easy to dip in and out of. I found the approach enjoyable to complete as well as being extremely powerful in terms of my professional development as a senior leader. My coachee found that our meetings helped her to lead significant improvements within our EYFS setting whilst also developing her skills as a senior leader. Our SLT are now planning on rolling out a coaching programme across the school using the online training with the wider school community."

Bronya Patmore, Deputy Headteacher, Brinkley Grove Primary School

"Excellent CPD for a number of staff that has had impact across the whole school."

Wendy Wallace, Headteacher, Crow Lane Primary School

"Learning to coach effectively has yielded rewards that reach way beyond individual conversations. Developing attentive listening skills, effective questioning techniques and an understanding of what motivates others is vital for anyone communicating with people. Unlike other coaching courses, Annie teaches these skills as well as imparting a genuine understanding of how coaching works and how it can help others. It has been enormously rewarding to see students and colleagues face challenges with renewed enthusiasm and increased effectiveness as a result of using the techniques in Annie's program. Put simply, this course will help unlock the potential in others."

Belinda Sorensen, Head of Campbell House & Careers Counsellor
Scotch College Adelaide, Australia

"Central to Annie's coaching model is a real sense of professional trust that is surely the heartbeat of every great school."

Joe Richardson, CEO, St Alban Catholic Academies Trust & Headteacher,
Cardinal Newman Catholic School

"Just incredible!...It's helped me to feel less stressed. It's made a really big difference, and I find it really gets much quicker results."

Suzette Mondroit, Senior Academic Coach, Passmores Academy ("Educating Essex" TV Series)

"It was very awe-inspiring as the programme went through, seeing how just wording different things, and just small steps, made an impact on members of staff straight away. The actual coaching team developed a relationship that supported each other, and that had an impact itself on each of our departments in the wider school. It was the best CPD. The one that has had the most impact. I've been teaching here nearly 10 years and it's been the best CPD that I've done. The one that you've come back from and said "Oh yes! - This is going to change things." Not the one you come back from and you throw the notes in the bin – "I've had a nice day out and I've had a nice lunch!" – The one that I knew was going to have an effect."

Carol Murray, Coaching Co-ordinator, Salford City Academy

"The most valuable training I've ever done, it has long lasting impact on both professional and personal life."

Elaine White, Director of Green Light Teaching School Alliance, Shelley College

"It helps you to make little changes which make big differences."

Stuart Foster, PE Teacher, Cowley Language College

"No one prepared me for the fact that a 3 day course would change my life! Coaching not only enhanced my career professional development but also my personal life… it works miracles!"

Lisa Gregson, Head of Key Stage 4, Queen Ethelburga's Collegiate

"I have seen the percentage of good teaching in school rise from 17% when I started to 43% after 7 weeks."

Sally Simpson, Headteacher, Parkland Infant School

"The skills and techniques covered and learnt through the *Coaching in Schools*" programme have had a significant impact on me. Professionally, within my leadership roles, I am better equipped to support staff without taking on extra work by guiding them to the solutions of their own problems. In my classroom, the subtle changes in the questions I ask have enabled students to become even more independent learners. Despite this being amazing, coaching has probably had its most profound impact on a personal level where I have used the approach of "small goals" to prevent myself being overwhelmed after I received the devastating news that a loved one had a terminal illness. Thank you, Annie and *Coaching in Schools*."

Gemma Kelly, Lead Teacher for Maths and Professional Learning,
Oak Grove College

ABOUT THE AUTHOR

Annie Boate is a highly qualified corporate coach and former teacher who's shaken up the coaching profession and put **coaching in schools** on the map! Her background includes various school leadership roles, working with young offenders and successfully coaching everyone from top executives in large international companies to outstanding Headteachers, and some of the most challenging learners.

As a full-time professional coach in schools, Annie's expertise is second to none, and her knowledge and enthusiasm instantly mark her out as being different. Spend a few minutes with her and you'll leave buzzing with practical, down-to-earth tools and ideas to use immediately.

Annie spent 18 years learning from some of the best coaches on the planet and developing a new, clever way of coaching for busy people in schools. This unique coaching system has been tested worldwide by new and experienced coaches, school leaders, teachers and support staff, and is proven to consistently out-perform all other models. Annie's work has been show-cased on TV, and is frequently described as "life-changing" and "transformational." It's reduced stress, boosted confidence and dramatically improved leadership, teaching & learning and results. *(Ofsted and school data verify this).*

You can see the impact and benefits for yourself in the case study interviews, success stories and reviews on coachinginschools.com or call 01636 351352 for more information.

Register for your free bonus gift

"The 10 Common Mistakes Schools Make When Developing Coaching – And How To Avoid Them!"

www.coachinginschools.com/book-offer

ACKNOWLEDGEMENTS

This book is for all the people who have allowed me to start '*A Coaching Revolution*' in their school.

Many people are afraid to risk doing things differently, so I want to acknowledge and thank the Academy Trusts, Headteachers and senior leaders who have believed in me and been brave enough to embrace this new way of coaching. Without your support we couldn't have made such a difference to so many people in schools worldwide.

To all of the amazing Accredited Trainers I'm lucky enough to work with. Thanks to your passion, commitment and hard work, thousands of extra people have been able to catch the 'coaching bug' and achieve better results in their work and personal lives.

To all of our trainee and graduate coaches for putting your learning into practice and helping so many of your colleagues, learners, friends and family to make changes and achieve their goals. I'm inspired, moved and humbled by your stories every day.

I also want to thank my family, friends, coaches and mentors who recently supported me through some very challenging personal times, kept me on track, and gave me helpful kicks up the behind! – You know who you are, and I will be eternally grateful to you.

Finally, I want to thank YOU for being willing to learn, develop yourself, and help your colleagues and learners to become even better. I'm extremely grateful to you for that, and for allowing me to be part of this transformational journey.

Annie

To Jill,

Thank you for your support & good luck in your retirement.

Annie x

A COACHING REVOLUTION

THE *NEW* CLEVER WAY TO COACH FOR TIME-STRAPPED
SCHOOL LEADERS, TEACHERS & SUPPORT STAFF

ANNIE BOATE

FOREWORD BY MONICA AUSTIN, HEADTEACHER

ISBN: 978-0-9955656-7-8

Published by Coachinginschools.com Publishing. First published in 2018.

CONTENTS

Foreword by Monica Austin (Headteacher)   17

Introduction   19

1 - Getting Started   35

2 - The Importance of Developing Your Core Skills   65

3 - How to Build Rapport Quickly & Easily   73

4 - How to Avoid Asking the 'Wrong' Questions   87

5 - Shut Up & Listen!   111

6 - Developing Your Model for Success   129

7 - Quick Wins for Instant Success When Coaching   149

Case Study: Ashcroft High School   173

FOREWORD

The success of coaching at Ashcroft still amazes me. I've been a Headteacher for fourteen years and I've come across coaching before, but never anything as powerful as this!

I've become a personal fan of Annie's work because using her coaching system and training at my school has had a massive impact on the school culture, the quality of leadership, staff development at all levels, students' academic progress and behaviour, school self-evaluation, staff recruitment… and the list goes on! You'll see my exact strategy for establishing our own Coaching Revolution in the Ashcroft High School case study at the end of this book.

If you want to know how to bring out the best in people in your school, and raise standards in an efficient and sustainable way, then 'A Coaching Revolution' is a trusted guide. Anyone who reads this book and applies what they learn in it, is bound to become a better leader, teacher or member of the support team – and it will change the way you work forever!

I hope that you enjoy what you discover in this book, and that your colleagues, your pupils, and your school benefit from Annie's simple but powerful coaching system as we have at Ashcroft.

I fully endorse Annie's coaching training and cannot recommend it highly enough.

Monica Austin, Headteacher.

INTRODUCTION

WHAT IS 'A COACHING REVOLUTION'?

If you've opened this book it may be because you want to develop coaching in your school, embed it, or turn it from 'good' to 'great'.

Coaching has been around for a long time now, and a lot of schools are doing it the old, traditional way, which sadly means they can never make as much impact as those schools who have implemented this latest best practice.

'A *Coaching Revolution*' takes place when the principles of effective coaching are applied to all aspects of school life. This includes an effective coaching system, underpinned by a powerful coaching model. The school adopts a coaching approach in everything that it does. It's an attitude. A way of working. A way of life.

WHAT DOES 'A COACHING REVOLUTION' LOOK LIKE IN SCHOOLS?

In schools where 'A Coaching Revolution' has taken place, people talk differently, think differently and behave differently. They're far more confident, motivated and empowered – and far less stressed! They approach problems differently. They're more productive. They get promoted. They manage their time and workload more efficiently, and they achieve seemingly insurmountable goals quickly and easily.

Inside the classroom there's better questioning, better teaching, and better progress. Aspirations are higher. Attendance is better. Behaviour is better. Learners are more engaged and more independent. They feel enthused, stretched and challenged. They understand things more deeply, recall information more easily, and achieve better results.

School leaders who are part of the revolution use coaching as a major strategy for improvement. They constantly 'walk the talk' by responding to daily incidents (with staff, parents and learners) using a coach approach. It's an integral part of their strategic planning, line management meetings and lesson feedback. Their teams feel inspired, supported and challenged. Meetings are more creative and productive. Working relationships are better. Communication is better. People perform better. They retain their best staff, and accomplish their improvement plan targets.

If you've come across 'coaching' before, (perhaps through sport or courses like the Outstanding Teacher Programme and NPQH), you'll find that this type of coaching is very different; it's a new, clever way of doing it, which is far more powerful, time-efficient and effective, so it's probably not coaching as you know it (unless we've met or you've done our training). Executive Headteacher Lesley Gwinnett sums this up beautifully when she describes the development of coaching, and the difference it's made at Tarleton Academy in her case study interview, 'The Silent Revolution' which inspired the title of this book. She says:

"Having been on the edges of coaching, especially with the Secondary Strategy, I knew that coaching was a fantastic tool. But even working in coaching with the Secondary Strategy I hadn't seen anything that was as transformational as this [coachinginschools.com training] seemed to be.

"I wanted these guys trained as trainers so that as many people as possible in our school can benefit from it, and we would have what we're calling this 'Silent Revolution', where just bit by bit by bit people have got the badge. And I mean got the badge. Literally putting the badge on…and being part of this almost 'secret society' that others are wanting to then be a part of. So it's not anything that we're forcing down people's throats. It's not anything that we've stood up in September 2012 and said, "Right – you're all doing this!" It's just got its own momentum that's just making such a change. It's fantastic!

"And I think as well for me, it's seeing the confidence that's developed… In the classroom it's powerful enough, but it's literally about the way that we work professionally and personally, and I think that's what's been so powerful. It's people standing up and giving testimony to how it's changed their relationships…and it's quite transformational - I keep using that word, but that's because it is!

"It's so simple, but so powerful. And everybody who has gone through the programme has seen themselves change for the better, without even realising they needed to. It's developed, and it's enhanced, and it's empowered…and in that way it's a huge impact, but not a big 'in your face' kind of way. It's just happening.

"The reason for doing it, first and foremost, was to transform teaching and learning. What I wanted was a school where relationships enabled students to learn more independently, where people felt confident to step back and let children think for themselves. And that's what I wanted…That was the reason for doing it. And I think, therefore, for the school, we're ticking boxes without fabricating it.

It's just become a natural part of practice, which means it's not a case of me going in and saying to people, "You need to get people thinking for themselves more in classrooms!" – It's naturally happening for those who've actually gone through the coaching training. So that's the big driver in the first instance, and everything that comes out of that is a fantastic additional.

"What it's given us is a vehicle for change that makes it more sustainable because it's embedded in practice.

*"It's a real change, not just a change for that fad. **I think for the people who've gone through the coaching training – it's changed who they are for the rest of their lives."***

RESOURCE

'The Silent Revolution' at Tarleton Academy

If you'd like to watch the full Case Study Interview with Lesley Gwinnett and Jo Bacon, you can find it here:

www.coachinginschools.com/teaching-and-learning-coaching

WHAT YOU CAN EXPECT FROM THIS BOOK

This book is NOT for everyone! It's been written specifically for time-strapped school leaders, teachers and support staff who are positive, open-minded, and genuinely want to help their colleagues and learners to achieve greater success with less effort – FAST! *(It's not for people who are looking for loads of academic theory, or who are 'set in their ways' or not prepared to develop their practice…so please don't read it if that sounds like you!)*

This book is written in plain English. It 'cuts to the chase' using simple strategies, real-life stories and practical examples to illustrate concepts and make them easily doable. Some of the names have been changed to spare some people's blushes…but most haven't! This book also shows you how you can make your coaching as efficient and effective as possible and start *'A Coaching Revolution'* in your school – whatever level you're at – in order to improve pupil outcomes and get the best possible results.

Whether you're new to coaching or an experienced coach, this book will help you because, unlike other coaching books, it gives you expert advice and strategies which are proven to make the greatest possible impact in today's schools.

- If you're a **beginner**, this book will help you to understand the fundamentals and develop your core practical skills. It will also guide you through the tricky part – how to take this information and easily incorporate these simple, powerful techniques into your daily life so that they become a 'natural habit' for you.

- If you're more **advanced** and have got some coaching experience under your belt, this book will help you to hone your skills, work less hard and make more impact in your coaching so that you get even more powerful results that you're really proud of.

- And if you're a **school leader** or **in charge of leading coaching** in your school, this book will give you tips, ideas, and a logical

25

strategic plan for developing and embedding coaching in your school with maximum impact and sustainability, using the **Best I.M.P.A.C.T. Blueprint®**

In fact, you can expect to use this information in all sorts of ways, just like Jo Bacon (Deputy Headteacher & Director of School Improvement at Endeavour Learning Trust) did. She says:

"I was very, very sceptical before I went on the [coachinginschools.com training] course. I'd just returned from maternity leave and I needed something to get my teeth into. And it was totally transformational for my teaching, my personal life and my managerial skills…I've seen results within my classroom…students understand things better and want to learn in a different way. They want to know the knowledge rather than being spoon-fed. And it changed my teaching dramatically. I was always told that I was very good at questioning within a classroom, but it's changed it dramatically, and I think that it's one of my strengths – and it's down to the coaching programme.

"It's changed the way that I go into meetings. It's changed the way that other people behave in meetings, and it's made us a lot more productive – silently – 'The Silent Revolution.' But it's permeated in all ways. And other members of staff – teaching and non-teaching – they speak differently now.

"I apply it to everything that I do. And I break everything down, and nothing ever looks too much anymore – "ain't no mountain high enough!" Everything gets broken down, and I know now that I can face a lot of things, and I think that's what people get from it.

"In my first term coaching, I coached a Year 11 pupil, and we only did one coaching session. And it was about the January and she said, "I only need one. I can do this now, Miss!"

"She wasn't on for her GCSE results, and she got them at the end. And on Results Day she said, "Thanks for that little chat we had in January, Miss - it worked!" And if it just happens with that one pupil, think what you can do!

"It's been totally remarkable for me personally, and for the school. I cannot imagine the school without it. I cannot."

WHAT WILL YOU LEARN?

When you read this book, you'll learn what you need to do to set up a powerful coaching system in your school, make it work 100% effectively, and stop it fizzling out. I'll share insider information with you, and give you plenty of useful advice, tips and tools which you can start using instantly to help make your job (and your life!) a lot easier. You'll discover:

- What theory you need to start coaching (so you don't waste your time with the unnecessary stuff!)

- What coaching REALLY is (it's not what 90% of schools are doing!)

- Why providing the solution rarely produces real or lasting changes

- What 3 things you need to be outstanding at to coach effectively

- How to stay clear of the 7 types of questions that will instantly kill your coaching and waste your time

- What 5 crucial ingredients make up a powerful question

- What 3 magic words you MUST use if you don't want to 'turn off' your coachee

- The 5 crucial things you need to do to fine-tune your listening

- What 6 things you need to listen for beneath the surface

- The 3 responses that will increase your rapport, gain you instant credibility and accelerate your coachee's progress

- Why 'old' models like GROW, TGROW, OUTCOMES, COACH, OSKAR, STRIDE and CEDAR set off alarm bells and don't work effectively

- Why a good coaching model will save you LOTS of time and stress

- How my '12-Step Model' **evolved** and why it **outperforms** other coaching models

- 10 'quick wins' to shortcut your success

- The 'Best I.M.P.A.C.T. Blueprint'® step-by-step roadmap that you need to follow to introduce and embed coaching effectively

So, as you can see, by the end of this book you'll know all of the basics and you'll have a really solid foundation to build on if you decide to take your coaching to the next level – this is vital if you want to maximise your impact and achieve far more powerful results.

WHAT YOU SHOULD NOT EXPECT FROM THIS BOOK

What I can't do in this book is make you into a truly outstanding coach, because that takes several months and requires further training in the '12-Step Model' and more advanced coaching skills. Without this training you'd make lots of mistakes, and you could easily cause some serious damage, so it would be totally irresponsible and unfair of me to put you and your coachees in that position. However, if it's something you'd like to learn, I'd love to teach it to you via the online or face-to-face training, so just email me [annie@coachinginschools.com] if you're interested.

MY COACHING JOURNEY

Have you ever felt like you wanted to make a difference to other people?

If you'd been there with me in 1998 you'd have seen me making a difference.

I'm a Head of Department and PE teacher in a deprived area. I don't know if you can relate, but I'm in the classroom facing eight very challenging, low ability 14-15 year old boys, who are bombarding me with questions like:

"Miss, why do we have to do this theory stuff?"

"Sir's a #@?*$!% idiot, Miss. This is such a #@?*$!% waste of time! Why can't he let us go and play football instead?"

"This school's stupid! What's the point of them making us do this? We're only going to #@?*$!% fail!"

"Yes, you're absolutely right, Andrew – you WILL fail if you've got that attitude. But if you're prepared to try, I reckon you can all get a decent grade, and that'll probably help you in the future. So, it's up to you!"

"Are you serious, Miss?"

"Yes"

"No way!"

"What? You really think we can pass?"

"Are you winding us up, Miss?"

"Listen boys, I've got an idea, so if you're prepared to try doing things a bit differently, and put some extra time and effort in, then so am I."

I look around the room at their stunned expressions.

What the hell have I just promised them? These 'disengaged' boys are predicted 'Fs' and 'Gs' in everything! Can they REALLY do any better than that, or am I in cloud cuckoo land?

I admit it's a long shot, but I have to try. I desperately want to help them escape the poverty trap. I want to boost their self-esteem, raise their aspirations and increase their confidence. And I'm convinced that a decent GCSE grade might just be the springboard to a better future for them, so I run my idea past Simon, the Head of PE.

"Annie, it sounds good, but let's be honest, the odds are totally stacked against you...These are some of the thickest kids in the school!"

"Yes I know, Simon, but I've been reading up on coaching and accelerated learning to help me in my Head of Department role. It's worked quite well with some of the people I line manage, so I thought I'd give it a go with this class."

"Well good luck then...I think you're going to need it!"

Over the next few months I take the knowledge I've accumulated and combine it into a simple, straight-forward coaching process to boost their confidence and help them recall things easily, ready for the big test of the GCSE.

I soon realise that my initial fears of, "what if it doesn't work?" or, "what if they won't engage with it?" were wildly wrong! The boys are already far more confident and motivated, their coursework grades have improved and, amazingly, they genuinely seem to believe that they CAN get a 'C' or above!

I'm elated!

A few weeks later, I enter the classroom and see eight despondent faces. Steven, a 6-foot lad with short, dark, wavy hair and freckles is in tears.

"What's up, lads?"

"Miss - it's not fair! We've just been given our exams list and we haven't been entered for the higher paper!"

I'm visibly shocked. "Really?!"

"Yeah. And that means we can't get a 'C', doesn't it?!"

"Yeah......Let me see that list, Steven."

"But you told us we could get a 'C', Miss. It's not fair. We've worked really hard! Can't you tell Sir to enter us? Otherwise we won't have a chance!"

I don't know if you've ever felt like you need to fight for something, but at that moment I knew I had to fight for these kids. So I approach Simon again:

"Simon, I've just found out that my group aren't entered for the higher paper."

"Don't be stupid, Annie! These kids can't even read properly. It's a complete waste of money. There's no way they'll get a C!"

"I honestly think they can. I'll even pay for it myself if that's what it takes? Simon, please! Just imagine how achieving just one 'C' grade could potentially change their lives."

To cut a long story short, after a bit of a battle, Simon agrees to enter them. I know I've made myself pretty unpopular, but I feel it was worth it because my boys now have the opportunity they deserve.

A few months later, I'm waiting nervously when the results finally come in:

1 x B (for a dyslexic boy), 4 x Cs, 2 x Ds and 1 x E

I cry with relief! You can imagine how proud I am of them. The battle was worth it. I've developed version 1.0 of the coaching system and tested it for proof. Today the system is radically different, and in Chapter 6 you'll see how I developed it further, but suffice to say I've now caught the 'coaching bug' and I'm hungry for more! So, I spend the next few years learning 'corporate coaching' from some of the best coaches on the planet, and adapting it for schools. I'm shocked that it's not as easy as I think it's going to be – surely as a 'teacher' and qualified coach in a range of sports this'll be second nature for me?!

Ha! I couldn't be more wrong! I'm absolutely rubbish at it at first, and I wonder if I should give up, but I decide to stick with it, because I really want to do a better job in developing the sixteen members of staff I'm now line-managing, having been promoted again in my new school. I want to help them, and as many pupils as possible, to overcome their challenges, to do better, and to feel better. So, I coach everyone I can, and just like my GCSE group improved, these new coachees are improving, and starting to believe in themselves too. I'm absolutely buzzing! In fact, I'm loving coaching so much that I desperately want to do it more, so I decide to leave education and enter the business world.

So here I am, sitting at my office desk, wearing my grey Armani suit. I've got a wardrobe full of designer clothes, a shiny new silver 4x4 on my drive, and I'm earning a pretty good living for someone my age.

I'm coaching powerful CEOs and Company Directors, and they're making really good progress.

I'm living my dream, doing what I love, and making a difference.

But there's a problem.

I can't quite put my finger on it, but somehow it just doesn't feel right.

As I look across my desk at the leather-bound, gold-embossed certificate that says 'CCUI', 'ICF ACTP' and 'CCC' – "Certified Corporate Coach", it suddenly hits me like a thunderbolt – I'm making a difference, but I'm making a difference to the wrong people.

However, it's very lucrative, and I know I'm able to earn a fortune in the business world, (which is not possible in education), so does it really matter?

It does to me.

Forget the bank balance, I need to listen to my heart. I need to make a difference to the right people – people in schools.

After that epiphany moment, I returned to education and picked up where I'd left off, but with an even bigger vision: To make school improvement faster and easier for busy people in schools. My goal was (and still is) to help everyone in schools to feel better and perform better.

As word spread, demand grew. More and more schools asked me to train them to get the results that they were hearing about, and pretty soon I was getting WAY more requests for my coaching programme than I could handle. I knew my capacity was limited, so I documented the EXACT processes, systems and models I use to help schools to get out of 'special measures', turn around 'failing' teachers, and quickly improve results. I then recruited more trainers and developed an 'online' version of my flagship programme so that I could help more people around the globe – even if their time or budget was tight!

The response blew me away. Cynics were converted, my work was showcased on TV, and we were finalists for a prestigious national award in the **'Best Coaching Programme'** category alongside giants like Barclays, Freshfields Bruckhaus Deringer, and Wm Morrison Supermarkets Plc.

Fast-forward to today, and to be able to use this tremendous vehicle of coaching to go into schools and somehow be able to touch lives and make a difference to colleagues, learners and parents is the greatest blessing that anyone could have given me. And I want to continue to use coaching in whatever way I can to help as many people in schools as possible to work better and feel better.

This book is part of that mission. I decided to write it because it felt criminal not to share my knowledge and 'short-cuts' when I know how hard people in schools are working to move things forward – and how so many of them are missing out on the huge potential of this new, clever way of coaching. Please don't be one of them!

So let's get started. I hope that you enjoy the journey as you make a difference to the people you care about and leave a lasting legacy.

CHAPTER

1

GETTING STARTED

WHAT DO YOU NEED TO KNOW TO COACH EFFECTIVELY?

Contrary to popular belief, you don't need masses of theory to start coaching, but you do need some!

Now that's important because what I don't want you to do is waste your time with all of the unnecessary stuff – and believe me, there's a lot out there – things that you really don't want or need to know. Things that really won't improve or add value to your coaching.

So this chapter will reveal **SECRET #1: What 3 crucial things you need to know to coach effectively.** By the end of it, you'll have a solid foundation that will enable you to get started with your coaching. And that's really important because if you've got a good understanding of each of these 3 areas, it virtually guarantees that you'll get much more powerful results.

So let's cut to the chase! What exactly do you need to know to coach effectively?

Well, there are 3 crucial things you need to know and understand:

1. What coaching is (and what it isn't!)

2. How it works

3. How to do it!

Just imagine these 3 things were the legs on a 3-legged stool. Now just think to yourself – what would happen if you kicked one of those legs out?

You've probably guessed it – the stool would fall down, wouldn't it?

So that's important because if we missed out one of these areas, you wouldn't really be very effective at all, would you?

So this chapter will give you that absolutely solid foundation which you need to start coaching.

When you're ready, let's begin with the first one...

WHAT COACHING IS (AND WHAT IT ISN'T!)

It's critical that you really understand what coaching is (and what it isn't) so that you can communicate it clearly to your colleagues and – even more importantly – you can get it right!

The terms 'coaching' and 'mentoring' are now used extensively in schools but, as Ofsted verify - there's no common understanding of what these terms actually mean! That's because in the last few years, 'coaching' has become a bit of a 'buzz' word, and it almost seems as though everyone from the National College to the corner shop have jumped on the 'coaching and mentoring' bandwagon. As a result, many schools have misconceptions of 'coaching'. They genuinely believe that they know what coaching is, and they genuinely believe that they're doing it - when, in fact, what they're actually doing is mentoring, observing and commenting on a lesson, giving extra tuition, providing training, or perhaps demonstrating how to do something! The really sad thing is that this means they'll never be able to achieve the sort of results and impact that would be possible if they did it correctly.

In fact, only the other day I met staff who were really nervous about becoming coaches because they thought they had to sit in the back of classrooms (or perhaps watch a lesson remotely on a live webcam) and then criticise and instruct their colleagues. And, of course, they had the idea that their colleagues would see them as 'the enemy' and hate them! To be honest they were probably right! They probably would have done if they'd gone down that route! So you can imagine how incredibly relieved they were when I told them that coaching really does not mean that!

In several other schools (where coaching has failed), all teachers were put in pairs or triads and told: *"Right, you're coaching each other! Go and watch each other's lessons and then have a chat about it and come up with some next steps."*

That's NOT coaching! That's watching each other's lessons, giving feedback and having a professional dialogue.

So what exactly is coaching then?

Well, if you're one of those people who likes definitions, here's my definition of coaching for you:

Coaching is...

"A structured conversation where a trained coach partners valued people in school to help them take quicker, more effective action that moves them from where they are to where they want and need to go, without giving them advice."

Annie Boate

Now let's break that down and look at it in a bit more detail.

Firstly, coaching is a **structured conversation**. In other words, there are certain things that you need to do in the right order, and that means working step by step through a model, like the **12-Step Model** that we teach in our programmes and online training course. (We'll talk more about models in Chapter 6). This structure keeps the conversation focused, productive and efficient. I imagine you're busy if you're anything like most people who work in schools, so if you're a bit worried about how long coaching takes, I can tell you that most people get through our 12-Step Model in around fifteen minutes, so I hope that reassures you a bit!

Secondly, a **trained coach**. Good coaches are not born, they're made! That's because coaching is not 'natural'. It goes against our 'normal' automatic behaviour and instinct a lot of the time, so unless we're trained to do this effectively, we simply won't get it right! We'll say the wrong thing, we'll get steps in the wrong order, and we'll miss critical things out. So the more you learn, the more you'll realise how much there is to learn, because unfortunately, coaching isn't as easy as it first sounds! In fact, that's why we build a practical skills assessment into our training at an early stage. Without this, we'd be setting trainee coaches up for failure, as people genuinely think that they're getting it right and don't realise that they've developed some 'bad habits' which could become ingrained! So it's critical that you master the skills properly and become aware of your bad habits, so that you can break them at an early stage.

The next point – **valued people**. Let's be honest, you are not going to waste your time with people who you don't value, so it's really important that when you start coaching, people realise the reason you're asking to coach them is because you value them, and you believe that they can work even more effectively (and help their department and school to achieve even higher levels of performance).

Fourthly, it's also about helping your coachee to **take quicker, more effective action**. Very often people procrastinate. They worry. And they end up taking slow action or no action!

I don't know if you can relate, but if you're anything like most busy people in schools, you'll have at least one BIG thing on your 'To Do' list that's been there for ages. It's like a dull ache that's been going on for weeks, months or even years. You keep pushing it to the back of your mind and putting it off, because in your head it feels like a massive and seemingly insurmountable mountain to climb.

In fact, you might even feel so daunted and overwhelmed by this task that you're not 100% sure where to start, so you either dive in without thinking it through properly or you stick your head in the sand and keep trying to avoid it!

You tell yourself you'll get around to it one day. Perhaps in the next school holiday? The problem is that there are so many other things on your 'To Do' list that you simply can't do everything. Nor can you do anything as well as you'd like to. You feel like you're spending a lot of time 'doing', but you're not achieving much or making as much progress as you'd like to. It's frustrating, demoralising and soul-destroying. I know because I've been there. And I also know that if you don't do anything about this you'll constantly feel overworked, tired and stressed, and then your health and home life will suffer. You may even burn out and lose your job.

It's the same for your coachee, and the problem is that this approach is the 'slow and ineffective' way to work. If they dive in without taking time to think, it'll actually take them a lot longer. And if they keep avoiding it (by filling their time with other things instead) then the dull ache gets worse; it takes up valuable 'head space' which slows them down and reduces their productivity.

Good coaching breaks this negative pattern; it'll enable you to take quicker, more effective action because you're actually taking time to 'disconnect' from everything around you and free up your mind to think! And when you're asked the right questions, you'll be able to come up with better ideas and insights which will help you to achieve your goal more quickly and easily than you'd initially thought.

By the way, in case you or your coachee(s) are worried that you're 'too busy' and haven't got the time to stop and think, I've got some good news for you: research shows that every minute you spend thinking/planning saves you as many as ten minutes in 'doing' or taking action. To put this in context, it only takes about 15 minutes to be coached using our 12-step model, so this tiny investment of time will increase your productivity and save you up to two and a half hours (150 minutes) in wasted time, energy and effort.

As well as helping people to work more efficiently and effectively, good coaching will move people from the point **where they are now** to **where they want and need to go**. Notice the focus on the future and moving forward. The point that the person wants and needs to get to could be anything! For example, it might be managing workload effectively, better time management, getting a promotion, moving teaching from 'good' to 'outstanding' or from 'requires improvement' to 'good', managing behaviour more effectively, increasing attendance, developing leadership skills, improving pupil progress, raising grades, increasing progress 8 score, school improvement planning, preparation for Ofsted, post-Ofsted action planning, improving confidence, reducing stress or better questioning in the classroom... etc.

Whatever the goal is, *how* they get there doesn't matter. It's the fact that they've got there that's the important thing.

Let me give you an example:

Think back to the last time you went on holiday.

Remember it?

Well, I bet that morning before you set off, you woke up in your bed or somebody else's bed – am I right?

Now think – what destination did you have to get to for your holiday?

OK, now I want you to be as creative as you can, and come up with 10 different ways that you <u>could</u> have got from your bed to that place that you were going on holiday. *(Pause for a minute to note down your 10 ideas in the space below!)*

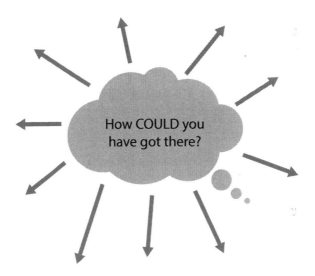

I hope you've come up with some really good, creative ways! You could have absolutely anything! For example, you could have perhaps walked, ridden a bike, got a taxi, ferry, train or bus, gone on a space hopper, roller skates, hopped, jumped, crawled, skipped etc... And, of course, you could have any combination of ways as well. I know that some ideas might sound ridiculous, but here's the thing - they still could have worked if you'd planned to use them.

OK, now think back to the way you actually picked to get to your holiday destination.

I bet that you picked the way to get there that you thought was best and easiest for you – am I right?

Of course, it might not have worked out that way because sometimes there are things like traffic jams that perhaps we hadn't planned for! However, if you're anything like most people, you'll tend to look at the options and then pick the way that's best and easiest for you to get to that point.

It's exactly the same for your coachees. And, by the way, that can be really hard for us as a coach to block out, because we have to remember that HOW they get to that point has to be the best way for THEM. It doesn't matter if it's our best way or not!

So to become a highly effective coach you don't need to know the answers, because you won't be **giving them advice**.

You might be totally shocked at that.

You might be thinking to yourself *"But Annie, how on earth can I coach somebody if I don't know the answers?"*

I'll let you into a secret – that was my first thought when I was asked to coach the Managing Director of a large industrial boiler company in the Netherlands. Despite my 3 years of corporate coach training I panicked! What did I know about industrial hot water boilers? (Zilch!) So how on earth could I coach this man effectively?

The answer was actually very simple. The way that I coached him was by becoming good at asking powerful questions so that he could find the answers himself. And that's all you need to do! You don't need to be the expert. In fact, it's actually a lot harder if you are an expert in the field because you're far more likely to make assumptions or start giving advice. Bear that in mind because otherwise, when you're coaching, you'll tend to ask questions that steer your coachee down the path to your best answer – not their best answer – and that's dangerous because you could actually inadvertently set them up for failure!

Remember, the critical point here is: HOW they get there really DOESN'T MATTER. It's the fact that they've got there that's the important thing.

So let's just sum it all up…

Coaching is:

Asking questions... listening... keeping the conversation focused... helping them to identify & set goals... focusing on solutions... following up & holding them accountable... and getting them to take action to achieve goals.

And coaching certainly isn't:

Touchy-feely... time-consuming... telling... suggesting... giving advice or guidance... teaching... training... instructing... observing a lesson and giving feedback... demonstrating how to do something... counselling... psychotherapy... letting them go off on tangents... setting goals for them... focusing on problems... leaving them to get on with it... OR EVEN WORSE – doing it for them!

WHAT'S THE DIFFERENCE BETWEEN 'COACHING' AND 'MENTORING'?

The second thing we need to know in terms of **what coaching is (and what it isn't!)** is what's the difference between 'coaching' and 'mentoring'?

These two words tend to be used together a lot – almost interchangeably at times – and that has caused a lot of confusion. So let's compare the two – what's the difference between mentoring and what a mentor does, and 'coaching' and what a coach does?

Let's have a look. It's actually quite simple.

A 'mentor' is usually an expert in the same field, often an experienced colleague in a more senior role, who provides advice and suggests ways of solving problems based on their experience and expertise. So your mentor might come along and say something like: *"Try doing this, that's what's worked for me!"* or *"Come and watch my lesson, and then go and do it in your class the same way that I do it."*

The coach on the other hand wouldn't do that, because what the coach would do – rather than providing advice and suggesting things – is ask questions to help the person find the solution that's best for them. So rather than focusing on the problem, the coach will be focusing much more on the solution, outcome and the way forward.

Let's say, for example, if a pupil has been misbehaving in a lesson, or if your colleague has made a mistake, what's the point of saying to them: *"Why did you do that?"* and focusing on the problem? (After all, most of them probably wouldn't have a clue – it just seemed like a good idea at the time!)

Would you agree that it's actually a lot more helpful to say: *"What could you do to stop that happening again?"*

The solution-focused conversation that emerges from the second question is far more likely to change behaviour, because you're forcing them to face up to it and deal with it. In my experience of working with people, that's a far more useful and productive approach than having a negative (and probably confrontational) discussion around why they did it!

Other bonuses I've found are that it forces people to take more responsibility for their actions and behaviour, and it builds those critical working relationships.

Something else to bear in mind is that you'll always get what you focus on. (So if you're focusing on problems, you'll get problems!) In fact, you've probably noticed how draining and exhausting it feels when you're around someone who's being really negative and problem-focused. It's like they're sucking all the positive energy out of you, so you'll obviously want to avoid this happening at all costs during your coaching meetings! Unfortunately, it's not always that easy, as lots of coaching models facilitate these 'energy vampires' by encouraging you to delve into the problem!

Here's what you need to do instead:

In an interview with SUCCESS magazine, when world champion racing driver Mario Andretti was asked for his number one tip for success in race car driving, he said: *"Don't look at the wall. Your car goes where your eyes go."*

This is one of the most crucial lessons to remember when you're developing coaching. In EVERY session, make sure you focus on the solutions (or road) ahead. If you focus on problems (the wall), then you'll waste time, depress your coachee and increase the chances of them hitting it!

THE 3 KEY DIFFERENCES BETWEEN 'COACHING' AND 'MENTORING'

Let's have a look at the 3 key differences between 'coaching' and 'mentoring'.

1. 'ASKS' –VS– 'TELLS'

The coach asks; the coach doesn't tell! And that can be quite hard, especially if you're thinking *"The answer is just soooo obvious...it's staring you in the face...why can't you see it?!"*

Obviously, the danger here is that you're likely to steer them down the path to your best answer, and that's not necessarily the best answer for your coachee.

Let me give you an example – Have you ever had a situation where you've had a bit of a problem or a dilemma, and you're not quite sure what to do about this thing?

And have you ever then gone and spoken to a friend or a colleague about it?

Well if your friends or colleagues are anything like mine you probably tell them whatever it is, and they listen, and then, because they want to help, they probably respond by saying something like: *"You should try...(such and such)"* or *"I know exactly what you mean – that happened to me and what you should do is..."* (And they give you a suggestion or little piece of advice).

Does that sound familiar?

And does that suggestion or advice ALWAYS feel like it's the best answer for you?

Probably not!

How come?

Well, it's simply because we're all unique, so what works for me isn't necessarily going to work for you, nor is it necessarily going to work for your coachee. So because we're all different, it's much more effective to 'ask' rather than 'tell' so that our coachees can find the answer that's best for them.

Think about it:

2 + 2 = 4
But so does 1 + 3
And so does 0 + 4

In other words, there's rarely only one way to do something, so let your coachee do it their way!

And remember…

"Telling creates resistance. Asking creates relationships."

Andrew Sobel

That leads me nicely onto the second key difference between 'coaching' and 'mentoring':

2. 'THEY SOLVE' –VS– 'YOU SOLVE'

Be honest – are you a bit of a 'fixer' or 'rescuer' or 'spoon-feeder'? Whether you are or not, you probably see it going on around you quite a lot. This 'mentoring' style approach is interesting because we think we're helping by solving it for them, but it's actually incredibly time consuming, exhausting and unsustainable for us.

Let me give you an example – Imagine I've got a problem and I'm not quite sure what to do about this thing, so I come to you and I tell you whatever my problem is. And imagine you give me some advice or a suggestion, so I thank you, and off I go, and I do whatever it is you've just told me to do…and it works! Fantastic! Thank you! ;-)

And then imagine a couple of weeks later I've got another problem – what do you think I'm going to do?

The chances are that I'll come back to you and present you with my new problem, and again expect you to solve it for me by giving me an idea, some advice or a suggestion. So, as you can see, I'm actually going to take up a lot of your time and become incredibly dependent on you…and it's going to be really hard for you to wean me off!

By using a 'coach approach' you'll get your colleagues and pupils to start taking responsibility and become a lot more resourceful. That, in turn, builds their confidence and stops it being so time-consuming and draining for you!

I don't know if you've ever read it – there's a great book out there called 'The One Minute Manager Meets the Monkey.' If you haven't read it yet, it really is well worth a read. (I loved it because it's such an easy read!) Anyway, it talks about how when people come to us with a problem they've got a monkey on their back. The minute they talk to us about their problem the monkey takes one foot off their shoulder and puts one foot on our shoulder. Then the second we say to them: "OK, I'll look into it for you" the monkey climbs across onto our shoulders. And when people keep doing that day in, day out, pretty soon we end up with a whole room full of monkeys (other people's problems) that we're dealing with, so we haven't actually got much time to do our own work!

I don't know if that sounds familiar to you, but the idea of the 'coach approach' is that we do not want a room full of monkeys! Nor do we want monkeys on our backs! So, we're not going to take on any monkeys – we're going to try to keep the monkey on the other person's back. By doing that, they'll solve it for themselves, and as a result they'll become a lot more confident, independent and responsible.

This concept is particularly important for you if you find people constantly coming to you for answers (especially if it's for trivial things). That's because if you keep solving things for other people, it puts you under enormous pressure to always have the answers. And then you risk getting the blame if your solution doesn't work for them!

In her case study interview NLE (National Leader of Education) & Headteacher Cori Bateman explains how she successfully used this approach when providing support to a new Headteacher in another school:

"She knows that sometimes I could just solve the problem with a snap of the fingers. But I'd be solving the problem my way – the Chantry way – rather than solving it her way, her school's way. What I've found when I have been tempted to give the 'quick fix' answer is that she's delivered that answer differently to how I would have delivered it, so the outcome hasn't been the same. So, if I had taken my own action in the way I'd described it, I would have had a certain outcome (and have had!) But because she did it with a slight twist – so I've explained something and she's gone off and done it, slightly differently to how I feel I explained it – the outcome didn't quite work. And I guess that's been a lesson to me. That if I want

this to work, it has to work for her and for her school, so it needs to be her solution. It can't be my solution because it's not me doing it, and it's not my school it's happening in. So it becomes really obvious that coaching is the solution when you see your own solution failing because somebody else isn't delivering it your way. So it's all the more reason to be using coaching rather than telling somebody the answers!

"There were a few examples of where there was something lost in translation, and it just didn't come out quite the way I thought it was going to, because it wasn't done in the way I thought it would be done! This way it fits the school, and fits the school's needs, and hopefully improves their outcomes even further...because their results this year are almost double last year's."

So, as you can see, by taking the 'coach approach' Cori took the pressure off herself to come up with solutions, and yet she still made a really positive impact and achieved the desired outcomes.

By the way, if you'd like to watch the entire Case Study interview I did with Cori, you'll find it here:

www.coachinginschools.com/coaching-headteachers

The third key difference between 'coaching' and 'mentoring' is:

3. '80:20' –VS– '50:50'

In a 'normal' conversation or a 'mentoring' conversation, it tends to be fairly even. They say a bit, you say a bit, they say a bit, you say a bit, and so on. However, in a 'coaching' conversation it's 80:20 – so that's the minimum we need to aim for.

So what do you think we're going to be doing for 80% of the time?

If you guessed 'listening', you are absolutely right! We'll be listening for at least 80% of the conversation, and 20% of the time we'll be speaking or asking questions to help them solve something for themselves and find a way forward.

To wrap it up in a nutshell, think of 'mentoring' as "putting in" and 'coaching' as "drawing out".

TASK

Come up with your own 1 sentence definition of coaching
(Tip: Keep it simple & make sure it doesn't have the word
'problem' in it!)

_____

_____

Now that you're clear about what coaching is (and what it isn't!), the next thing you need to know to get started is how it actually works.

HOW COACHING WORKS

The key thing to remember is that the coachee is the one who drives the process. They're in the driving seat. It's always got to be their agenda, and they've got to have ownership and buy-in to the whole process. In other words, it's no good forcing someone to be coached or imposing a goal on them.

So, for example, if I told you that on Saturday I've arranged for a plane to go up and you're going to be on it. The plane will climb to 13,000 feet. You've got a parachute strapped to your back. At 13,000 feet, you're going to jump out of the plane. You're going to free-fall to 5,000 feet. At 5,000 feet, you're going to pull the rip cord, and then you've got to come down to land in a tank in a field – and in that tank are snakes, spiders and sick!

If I set that as your goal, how motivated would you be to actually do it?

Personally, I reckon that you'd have to be a little bit weird to want to land in a tank that's full of snakes, spiders and sick, don't you?! (That is, of course, if I didn't lose you before you even got on the plane!)

So as I said before – it's no good imposing a goal! By taking a 'coach approach' and letting them set the goal, you'll find that the change will come from them – rather than you. This means that they're internally motivated to take action to change, so you get faster improvement and long term improvement. In other words, if we have our 'mentor' hat on and tell people what to do, or we give advice, or use coercion, they'll do it for one of two reasons:

1. Because they like us and they want to please us!

OR

2. Because they they're frightened of us (and scared not to!)

So if they're doing it for one of those two reasons, then all of the time we're looking over their shoulder they'll keep doing it. But the moment that we step back (and we're not looking), what do you think is going to happen?

The chances are that they'll slip back into their old way of doing things because it's not their best way, it's our best way. And what works for us isn't necessarily going to work for them. We've all got our own best ideas, and just because it's our best idea, it doesn't mean that it's the right way for them. So in other words, a 'quick fix' 'providing the solution' (or mentoring) type approach rarely produces real or lasting changes. And the reason for that is firstly because no two people are alike, and secondly because the crucial 'inner motivation' to change simply isn't there. So people have got to 'want' to change and they've got to do it in the way that's best for them!

So if we can stop 'telling', 'suggesting' or 'advising' and start taking more of a 'coach approach' we'll be able to work more effectively and get faster, sustainable improvement. You just need to believe that they've got the answer locked away inside them, and ask powerful questions which will help them to unlock and discover it.

So now that you know what coaching is (and isn't!) and how it works, the third and final thing that you need to know to coach effectively is...

HOW TO DO IT

That's easy, because that's exactly what the rest of this book is about!

I'll be guiding you through one step at a time so you can gradually build up the fundamental skills that you need, learn some of my magic formula, and most importantly, find out how you can start 'A Coaching Revolution' so that you can help your colleagues and pupils to improve their performance – Fast!

I do have to warn you that there is a catch! You have to do it exactly the way I tell you for it to work. It's like any tool – if you use it correctly, it'll work well for you, and if you don't use it correctly, it can't possibly work as well as it should. So as you read this book, you'll begin to realise how powerful coaching can be when it's done properly and how easily it can fit in to your school.

What you then do next is entirely up to you, and it really depends on how well you want to do it. If you decide you want to do it really well, then by the end of this book you'll feel that you want to take your skills to the next level (so that you can get even more powerful results), in which case I'll be happy to talk to you about how you can do that, if you want to, and if it's right for you.

I'm also pretty sure that it'll come as no surprise to you that what you get out of this will depend on what you put in to it. If you want to be a really outstanding coach don't just 'do' coaching, 'become a coach' by practising, being coached and blending it into your everyday life at work and home so that it becomes 'second-nature'! A great free resource that can really help you with this is the weekly #coachingchallenge – it's published at 8:30pm on Sundays during term time. All you need to do is follow @schoolcoachguru on Twitter or search 'coaching in schools' on Facebook and 'like' the page to get it... then join in!

You now know all the theory that you need to know to get started with your coaching, so when you're ready, let's move onto the practical stuff!

Please take your time, work through this book at your own pace and make sure you're 100% confident with each skill or concept before you move on to the next one. If you'd like any help or advice along the way, you can get instant access to more than 150 online resources, videos and support at:

www.training.coachinginschools.com

or you can give me a ring on +44 (0)1636 351 352

SUMMARY

'Coaching' and 'mentoring' are very different and there are many misconceptions of 'coaching' in today's schools. Imposing goals or 'providing the solution' rarely produces real or lasting changes, whereas a genuine 'coach approach' means you'll be able to work far more effectively and get faster, sustainable improvement.

CHAPTER

2

THE IMPORTANCE OF DEVELOPING YOUR CORE SKILLS

Get instant access to over 150 online resources, videos and support at:

www.training.coachinginschools.com

THE IMPORTANCE OF DEVELOPING YOUR CORE SKILLS

Nobody can become a great coach without developing their core skills. The problem is, most of us naively assume that because we're educators, we're naturally brilliant at these things – I must confess that in my ignorance, that's exactly how I felt initially, because I simply didn't know what I didn't know. Funnily enough, the majority of our new trainee coaches feel the same way I did when they first come across these 'core skills' on our face-to-face or online training courses.

"People with a growth mindset believe that they can improve with effort. They outperform those with a fixed mindset, even when they have a lower IQ, because they embrace challenges, treating them as opportunities to learn something new."

Travis Bradberry

I'll let you into a secret – we track our programmes, and the coaches who have got the best results have done so because they made a conscious effort to master these core skills. This gave them a solid foundation to build on, which enabled them to become outstanding coaches. Now I don't know about you, but I certainly didn't pop out of my mum's womb as 'a coach'. In fact, I was absolutely rubbish at most of these skills when I first began. Fast-forward 18 years and I can now quickly spot 'coaching mistakes' and give my trainees practical tips to develop their core skills so that they get much better outcomes in their coaching and in the classroom. This often surprises them as they don't tend to realise that they've made a 'mistake' until it's pointed out to them, so they'll ask me, *"How on earth do you do that so quickly?"*

The answer is simple – practise, practise, practise!

Listen, I'm nothing special. I'm just an ex-teacher who's invested my time and money in learning from experts and practising the skills until they've become 'automatic' – and you can easily do the same.

Like all of our trainees, once you've mastered these critical core skills, you'll notice a dramatic improvement in your coaching impact and efficiency, and you'll also find that it makes a HUGE difference to your teaching, leadership and results.

Here's the truth – if you're anything like most people, your 'natural' behaviour won't always be the 'best' behaviour for coaching! However, if you keep repeating the 'new' alternative behaviour as often as possible, you'll make incremental improvements and you'll eventually master each skill and be well on your way to starting your own *Coaching Revolution*. By the way, if you're a bit worried about how long this will take you, don't panic! You can easily integrate these practical skills into your everyday work and life so that it's not 'extra' things for you to do; you'll just be doing the same thing in a different way until it becomes your 'natural' and 'auto-pilot' behaviour. That's really important, because if you're ever tired or stressed you'll always revert to your 'natural' behaviour, so practise, practise, practise, and remember:

"We are what we repeatedly do.
Excellence then, is not an act, but a habit."
Aristotle

Now if you're ready, let's reveal **SECRET #2: What 3 things you must be absolutely outstanding at to coach effectively.** Once you've got the hang of these skills, and see for yourself the difference they make, there will be no going back!

WHAT 3 THINGS DO YOU NEED TO BE OUTSTANDING AT TO COACH EFFECTIVELY?

In order to coach and improve performance fast, you need to be outstanding at:

1. Building rapport

2. Questioning (core skill)

3. Listening (core skill)

Before we look at these, here's a word of warning: Some people slip into a 'fixed mindset' when they hear the words 'rapport', 'questioning' and 'listening'. They start to roll their eyes and think to themselves, *"I work with children, I know this stuff – it's what I've been trained to do!"* Then they either 'switch off' or waste their time trying to prove and document their skills to anyone who will listen, rather than trying to develop and refine them! Do you know anyone like that?

Over 10,000 hours of observing lessons and coaching sessions in schools has convinced me that these skills do NOT come naturally to 99% of us, and it's only when someone draws our attention to our mistakes that we realise the truth! As a result, many coaching conversations, lessons and meetings lack the impact that they could have if the coach had chosen to have a 'growth mindset' and consciously cultivate their skills – if you can do this, you'll be well on your way to becoming an outstanding coach. Yes, it might be difficult. Yes, it might push you to the edge of your comfort zone at times, and yes, you might find some of these skills harder to develop than others. However, when you finally master them, it'll be well worth the effort, because if you're anything like most people, you'll be surprised at the phenomenal difference it makes to both your coaching and your everyday practice.

So when you're ready, let's begin with the first one – building rapport.

SUMMARY

When you get good coaching education and master the 'core skills' the quality of your coaching, teaching and leadership will be even better. And you'll get far better outcomes.

3

HOW TO BUILD
RAPPORT QUICKLY
& EASILY

Get instant access to over 150 online resources, videos and support at:
www.training.coachinginschools.com

BUILDING RAPPORT

If you want to coach your colleagues or learners to 'outstanding' and beyond, the very first thing you need to be able to do is build rapport effectively. In other words, you need to be able to connect with people and create a bond with them within the very first few minutes. This is important because people work better with people that they know, like and trust.

Remember:

*"Nobody cares how much you know,
until they know how much you care."*

Theodore Roosevelt

So, if you can become outstanding at building rapport, you'll build a strong relationship with your coachee that will put them at ease and make them feel that you really understand them. This creates a sense of trust, which means that they'll naturally become far more open with you and share more information. That will make your coaching far more productive and effective, and will dramatically accelerate your coachee's progress.

Just think for a minute...

- Have you ever met a perfect stranger for the first time and hit it off like a house on fire? You feel like you naturally 'click', and it's as if you've known them for years, even though it's perhaps only been a few minutes or hours. Have you ever experienced that?

- On the other hand, have you ever met someone and instantly disliked them, or felt a bit uncomfortable with them for no apparent reason? The conversation almost feels like you're pulling teeth, and you can't wait for it to be over. Have you ever had that?

Rapport usually happens naturally and subconsciously, so if we can understand how it works, we can then use this information to our advantage by making a conscious effort to do it. That, in turn, helps us to build really strong coaching relationships that will produce more rapid results.

So the question is: How can you create rapport with someone quickly and easily?

There are 3 key techniques that you can use:

1. Make A Positive First Impression

2. Find Common Ground

3. Copy and Lead

OK - Let's have a look at each of them in turn:

1. MAKE A POSITIVE FIRST IMPRESSION

You obviously don't get a second chance to make a first impression, so we need to make sure that our first impression is positive and that it counts. So here are some tips for you:

a) **Smile and say "hello" in a positive, upbeat way** – they will 'catch' this and hopefully then reflect it back to you by responding in the same way.

b) **Be positive** (avoid negative comments about anything or anyone!)

c) **Put your coachee and their needs first** – try to see the world through their eyes, understand their emotions, and really try to get 'on their level'.

d) **Be 100% passionate about wanting to help your coachee** – if you genuinely believe in your heart that your coaching will have a profound effect on your coachee, it will! And, of course, if you don't, it won't!

e) **Create the right environment:**

✓ **Find a good venue** for your coaching (this might be a room/ office in school or an external location) – the important thing is that it's neutral territory and you've got no interruptions. Interestingly, I remember Vic Goddard, Principal of Passmores Academy, telling me that he goes off-site to a coffee shop for his coaching to avoid being disturbed – I think that's a really smart tip for anyone in a leadership role!

✓ **Put a sign on the door!** – One of the training resources that you can download is a sign which is really clear in telling people not to enter the room (unless you need to evacuate the building!) It also gives clear instructions of what they need to do to contact you. The important thing is that people realise it does apply to them – whoever they are! By the way, it helps if you print it on bright yellow paper and put it at eye level above the door handle. Then, if someone does ignore it and walk in, look surprised, give them a 'stop' hand signal and calmly say: *"Sorry [first name] - This is a confidential meeting. Has the sign fallen off the door?"* – That tends to make them realise it does apply to them and stops them doing it again!

✓ **Stop all interruptions** – Make sure you do things like turning off your phone and iPad and shutting down your emails to stop them pinging in and disturbing you.

✓ **Make it as comfortable as possible**. Think about:

- Temperature

- Light

- Timing – What's the best time for your coachee? (Are they a 'morning person' or an 'afternoon person'? Would they prefer coaching in their non-contact time or lunchtime or before or after school?)

- Furniture – make sure it's the same height and there are no barriers. You can't coach effectively sat opposite somebody across a table because it feels more like an interview. You'll find it much more comfortable if you can position your chairs at about a 90° angle (ideally with a coffee table between you), because sideways on feels much less threatening so the person will relax and open up more.

- How close you're sitting – make sure chairs are a comfortable distance apart and don't invade their personal space!

- Can you provide refreshments? I don't know about you, but I find if I give most people a cup of tea and a chocolate biscuit they'll pretty much tell me anything! ;-)

- Taking off your ID badge – I thought it was a brilliant idea when one of our graduates, Amanda Cawood, told me that she takes her ID badge off when she enters the room so that she's seen as 'Amanda the coach', not 'Amanda the Deputy Head' (or 'Amanda the Headteacher' as she is now!) This action obviously reinforces the confidential and non-hierarchical nature of the coaching relationship too, so if you do this, it'll help to put your coachees at ease and get them to open up to you more quickly.

Once you've made a positive first impression, the second thing you can do to create rapport is:

2. FIND COMMON GROUND

The bottom line is that people like people who are like them, so it's much easier to 'click' with someone if you have something in common. If you can find some common ground, you'll both feel a sense of 'connection' that will create instant rapport between you, so ask open-ended questions to discover some personal information and find something that you both have in common. Perhaps you have lived in the same area, or have been to the same place on holiday. Perhaps you both know the same person, or maybe you support the same football team. It could be anything. Remember - ANY common ground can help establish rapport – so show an interest in your coachee's life or hobbies to create rapport and build your coaching relationship.

Once you've made a positive first impression and you've found some common ground the third thing that you can do is:

3. COPY and LEAD

One of the fastest ways to build rapport with another person is to 'match' or 'mirror' them! Matching or mirroring is when you adjust your own body language and spoken language so that they're the same as the person you're talking to. The everyday word for matching and mirroring is 'copying'. If you want to know the difference between the two, imagine you're opposite me and I lift my left arm up – to 'match' me you'd also lift your left arm up, whereas if you were 'mirroring' me you'd lift your right arm up (so it's like a reflection in a mirror).

Don't worry – we're not talking 'Simon Says' here! (You're going to leave a gap of about 10 seconds so it's not really obvious or embarrassing!) It might sound a bit daft, but if you look around you, you'll see that this is exactly what people do naturally all the time! So I'm going to ask you to make a conscious effort to do just that - look around you and notice how people copy each other's facial expressions, gestures and seating positions. See how if somebody raises their eyebrows, the other person raises theirs. Notice how if somebody smiles, the other person smiles back. See how when somebody puts their hand on their chin, the other person mirrors it. Also notice how they copy certain words, and the volume, tone, pitch and speed of the voice. Some people even accidentally copy accents – have you ever done that or do you know anybody who has? (I know I have!)

That's natural rapport.

TASK

Look out for 'matching' or 'mirroring' in the next 24 hours and make a note of at least 3 examples you spot!
(Tip: look for verbal & non-verbal things!)

1. _____

_____

2. _____

_____

3. _____

_____

OK, so what does all of this mean for you?

It means that if you make a conscious effort to copy your coachee, you'll speed-up the rapport-building process.

Once you've copied them for a few minutes, you'll then be able to take the 'lead' to get them into a productive state for the coaching session far more quickly and easily by perhaps adjusting your body language or the speed and volume that you're speaking at.

They will then copy you!

If they don't copy you, what do you think you'd need to do?

You'd simply need to copy them again, and then try to lead again! Hopefully this time they'll start copying you (even though they wouldn't be conscious of it). And if they don't, just keep repeating the process of copying and leading until they do!

Research suggests this is the most effective way to establish rapport so they become more receptive. It's very subtle, but it makes the other person feel comfortable and, most importantly, it makes them feel that they're being understood.

SUMMARY

Building rapport quickly enables you to get your coaching off to a flying start. It makes it far more productive and effective and helps you to dramatically accelerate your coachee's progress.

CHECKLIST

'Building Rapport' Quickly & Easily in Coaching

	Yes	No
1. Did you smile & say "hello" in a positive, upbeat way when your coachee arrived for their coaching session?		
2. Did you stay positive throughout the conversation?		
3. Did you avoid making any negative comments about anything or anyone?		
4. Did you put your coachee and their needs first ?		
5. Did you try to see the world through their eyes, understand their emotions, and really try to get 'on their level'?		
6. Were you 100% passionate about wanting to help your coachee?		
7. Did you genuinely believe in your heart that your coaching would have a profound effect on your coachee?		
8. Did you pick a suitable venue for your coaching?		
9. Did you put a 'no entry' sign on the door?		
10. Did you avoid all interruptions? *(eg people, phones, emails etc.)*		
11. Was the room temperature comfortable?		
12. Was there enough light in the room?		

	Yes	No
13. Was the session scheduled at the best time for your coachee?		
14. Were your chairs positioned at a 90° angle?		
15. Did you make sure there were no barriers (such as a table) between you?		
16. Were you sat a comfortable distance apart?		
17. Did you have refreshments?		
18. Did you take off your ID badge?		
19. Did you find some common ground?		
20. Did you copy (match & mirror) your coachee and take the lead when appropriate?		
TOTAL SCORES:		

What's ONE thing you could do to make your rapport even better?

_____

_____

HOW TO AVOID ASKING THE 'WRONG' QUESTIONS (CORE SKILL 1)

BRAIN BEFORE MOUTH!

As a coach you need to become absolutely outstanding at questioning. No matter how much you're tempted – ask questions only. No fixing. No leading. No suggesting. That's because questions are far more effective than answers in engaging people, promoting learning, and helping them to make much faster progress.

By asking powerful questions, you'll enable your coachees to think and discover things for themselves, which means that they are FAR more likely to remember it, understand it, and (where necessary) do something about it.

This will also help to build their confidence, self-esteem and resourcefulness for life.

So in this chapter, I'll share with you:

1. How to stay clear of the 7 types of questions that will instantly kill your coaching and waste your time (and be warned – you're probably doing at least 2 of these things right now!)

2. What 5 crucial ingredients help you to create a powerful question.

In fact, you'll probably be quite amazed at how hard it is to ask a powerful question because, whilst most of us think that we're pretty good at this, you'll realise this isn't something that's natural or instinctive. And believe it or not, it's NOT something that we tend to be very good at! (Although most of us tend to assume we are!)

Think of it like 'the human Google'. When you ask a question, it's just like entering a search term into Google – the brain will search through its 'files' for answers, and keep looking until it finds them! The funny thing is that you don't always realise it's doing it, but you know this is true if you've ever not been able to think of the answer to something straight away... and then it suddenly pops into your head several hours (or even days) later!

Has that ever happened to you?

The important thing to remember is to be careful what you ask, because just like with Google, if you ask rubbish questions you'll get rubbish answers/results!

Let me explain. Have you ever asked yourself something like: "Why am I so stupid?"

If you have, then your brain will have come up with a list of reasons/answers for why you're so stupid (which probably made you feel worse!) That's because the question would have led your to brain find answers which back up the belief that you're stupid!

As a coach, you obviously want to avoid asking rubbish questions, so please try to follow the tips I'll give you in this chapter and do what I call "brain before mouth!" In other words, get the question in your head and check that you're 100% happy with it BEFORE it comes out of your mouth!

Finally, don't slip into the trap of blaming the coachee if you're not getting the 'right' answers. I'll be blunt – it's not THEIR fault, it's yours! The bottom line is that you haven't asked the right question if that's the case! So what do you need to do?

Simply become outstanding at questioning so that you can ask a better question instead!

Now, if you're ready I'll show you exactly how to do that.

THE 7 TYPES OF QUESTIONS THAT WILL INSTANTLY KILL YOUR COACHING AND WASTE YOUR TIME

1. FOCUSING ON THE PROBLEM

This is hard because our natural response and instinct is to ask about the problem. Let me show you what I mean:

Imagine if I was your coachee and I said to you: "I'm stuck!" What's the first question that pops into your head?

If you're anything like most people your natural response would be to ask me something like: *"What are you stuck with?"*

Think about it – if you asked me this, what would you be focusing me on?

Being stuck. In other words the 'barrier' or the 'problem'. That's not helpful and it's not going to move me forwards.

In coaching we want to focus on the solution (not the barrier or problem), so it would be far more helpful if you asked me: *"What could you do to get unstuck?"* or: *"How could you get unstuck?"* because those questions will flip me from a negative problem focus to a positive solution focus, and that will help me to move forward.

Unfortunately, this tends to go against our natural instinct and our gut reaction. So, consider this – if you ask your coachee about the problem, what sort of frame of mind is this likely put them in?

The chances are it'll lead to the conversation going in a negative, downwards spiral, in which case it's highly unlikely that they'll feel motivated to take action to change! So if a question focuses on the problem, it can quickly and easily kill your coaching session, so you need to flip it into focusing on the solution instead!

> ## "Most people spend more time going around in problems than in trying to solve them."
>
> *Henry Ford*

2. CLOSED QUESTIONS

These usually start with words like:

- Are you...
- Could you...
- Can you...
- Do you...
- Is there...
- Have you...
- Would you...
- Will you...

These types of questions usually get a single word or very short, factual answer.

Imagine you wanted your coachee to think of some ideas for achieving their goal, and you asked them: *"Could you think of any more ideas?"*

What could your coachee say?

"No!"

What about if you asked: *"Have you got any other ideas?"*

Again, they could say: *"No!"*

How about if you asked: *"Can you give me another idea?"* or: *"Is there another idea?"* or: *"Do you think you can give me another idea?"*

Again, what could they say?

"No!"

So what your closed question has done is instantly shut off their thinking and disengaged them!

That's not helpful or productive for coaching (especially if you're working with someone who's a bit lazy or lacking in confidence), because the easy way out for most people is to say: "No." or: "I don't know!"

Unfortunately, the message people have got from years of programming is that if they say: "No." or: "I don't know!" they'll be let off the hook and someone will dive in and rescue them or fix it for them and they won't have to think any more!

If, on the other hand, they know that you expect an answer, and you ask them a nice open question like: *"What are three more ideas?"* you'll engage their brain and send it off looking for more answers. This will help them to come up with a far more effective response. So avoid questions that are closed as they will quickly and easily kill your coaching!

3. LEADING QUESTIONS

These types of questions make people feel forced or railroaded into agreeing and tend to produce an 'autopilot' response. There are two main types of leading questions. The first type is what I call:

- **The 'puppeteer'.** For example, if we say: *"Do you understand?"* or: *"Has anybody got any questions?"* or: *"Do you know what I mean?"* or: *"Are you OK with that?"* it's like we're pulling puppet strings – they obligingly nod and shake their heads in the right places to give us the response they think we're after!

But have they actually thought about it?

It's highly unlikely. It's just that automatic response that we're getting.

You've probably noticed this in the classroom. You explain the task and then ask something like: "Do you understand?" The class all nod their heads appropriately, so you ask them to get on with it. Then, a few minutes later, you notice some learners not doing it, and when you ask why they reply: "Because I'm not sure what to do!"

Does that sound familiar?

You can see how the autopilot response was generated – they knew that you expected the answer to be: "Yes." And so that's exactly what they said, without actually thinking about it!

The problem is with the way the question is structured. Whilst we don't mean it to sound like this, asking leading questions such as: "Do you understand?" implies that the onus is on the other person to understand what we're trying to tell them when, in fact, the onus should be on us (the communicator) to get the message across clearly.

As a result, when we ask them: "Do you understand?" what they hear is something like: "Is there anything you were too stupid to understand?!"

And let's be honest, who really wants to put their hand up and draw attention to themselves? It's like they're saying: "Yes, I'm the idiot who didn't get it the first time you explained it! Look at me everyone!"

A great tip to avoid this is to ask something like: *"What do I need to clarify or explain more?"* or: *"What do you need to ask so you can complete this successfully?"* instead of a leading question.

Try it and notice the massive difference it makes and how many more questions you get!

- **The 'influencer'.** Another type of leading question is suggesting something to plant an idea in your coachee's head. So you might say something like: *"How about if you asked someone?"* or: *"Why don't you go on the internet to look for some ideas?"* or: *"That's probably your best idea, isn't it?"* or: *"What if you tried it this way next time?"*

  Notice how these sorts of question force someone to agree, or influence them to think in a certain way, or point them to what we consider to be the 'right' answer – even though the chances are, it's not their best answer. So, as you can see, a leading question can kill the coaching because it takes away ownership, which means they are unlikely to do it or sustain it.

4. LIMITED CHOICES QUESTIONS

These questions give your coachee the alternative answers within the question. For example, if you asked them: *"Is it very difficult for you or is it OK?"* they'd probably say: *"Yes it's difficult"* or: *"No, it's OK"* – and you wouldn't get anywhere near as much information as if you'd asked you a more open question. Likewise, if you asked your coachee: *"Do you want to come up with 2 options or 4 options?"* you'd be forcing them to pick one of your answers and closing off alternative responses, which could effectively kill the coaching. What if they wanted to come up with 10 options?

5. IRRELEVANT INFORMATION-GATHERING QUESTIONS

A really common mistake for beginner coaches is to waste time gathering background information that they really don't 'need' to know to coach effectively! You don't need to be an expert in the field, and knowing more about something won't necessarily improve the quality of your coaching. In fact, it's likely to be a disadvantage as you're more likely to slip into advising and suggesting things! So avoid irrelevant information-gathering questions and just concentrate on helping your coachee to move forward and achieve their goal.

6. MULTIPLE QUESTIONS

This is when you stack up two or three questions together.

Let me ask you something - Do you suffer from premature articulation?

Most people do, because what happens is, we start asking a question before we really know what we want to say, so we end up tagging bits on or rephrasing it. Then, before we know it, the question has become very long and confusing or we've actually asked two or three questions at once! It happens a lot. In fact, if you ever watch the news or talk shows you'll often see the interviewer doing this. Look out for it and notice what effect this has on the answer they get!

Now let's think about you. Have you ever been to an interview and been asked one of those long questions that goes on and on and on forever, and they get to the end and you're sat there scratching your head thinking: "What on earth have they just asked me?"

Has that ever happened to you?

If it has, you'll have found that it overloads your brain, and by the time they get to the end you've missed the point or forgotten what they've asked you.

When this happens how does it make you feel?

Most people feel panicked, confused, stupid and stressed – so if we were to do that in coaching, you can understand why it could actually kill off the coaching conversation very easily! Instead, what we need to do is ask one short, sharp question so that people understand it the first time. That's particularly important if you ever work with somebody that's got attention deficit hyperactivity disorder (ADHD), speech and language difficulties, or perhaps a different first language to you. Long questions will confuse them, so keep it short and avoid stacking up multiple questions.

7. "WHY?" QUESTIONS

As a coach, you need to avoid: "Why" questions, since they can be counterproductive and can easily kill the coaching. "Why?" can be interpreted as accusatory, criticism or personal attack, especially if you use the wrong tone of voice or body language.

Take a minute to look at the examples below and think to yourself: "How do these questions actually sound?"

- *"Why did you do that?"*
- *"Why didn't you achieve that target?"*
- *"Why was this late?"*
- *"Why do you think that's a good idea?"*
- *"Why have you still got your coat on?"*

Now think: How could these sorts of questions make somebody feel?

They could make people feel stressed, defensive and like they have to justify their actions.

That's because – while we don't actually mean it like that, "Why" tends to convey judgment rather than curiosity; and accusations rather than observations. So "Why" questions very often result in a defensive, negative or perhaps even a sarcastic response which is unhelpful, time-wasting and can lead to confrontation and damaged self-esteem.

For instance, when we ask a coachee: *"Why did you try that idea?"*, the way that question is structured is counter-productive. They are likely to interpret that question as you saying you think the idea was a bad thing to do. It's pretty obvious that the coachee tried that idea because they believed it was a good one at the time. There isn't always a reason or motive. They might have been dead wrong, but they still believed they were doing the right thing at the time, by trying it. So, to your coachee, your "Why" question sounds like you're putting them down and can easily damage their confidence, their self-esteem and their self-worth.

"Why" questions can also foster some of the most sarcastic responses. For example, when I got my first iPhone, I'd had it literally three days and I was sitting drinking coffee and playing with it when all of a sudden, it slipped out of my hand into my cup of coffee!

I was mortified!

I felt sick!

And straight away, do you know what the person I was with asked me?

"Why did you do that?"

As you can imagine, I was livid! I felt like saying: *"What a stupid question!"* or *"Because I was bored and thought I'd just waste six hundred quid seeing if it would float!"*

Needless to say, that would have been unhelpful and unproductive, so I kept my mouth shut!

However, if the question asked was: *"How could you make sure it didn't slip in the future?"* then that would have definitely been far more helpful and productive!

The point is that we need to avoid the why questions that can trigger negative or sarcastic responses. So here's the secret - if you can change the negative "Why" into a more positive "What", "How" or "If" question, you'll generate more positive, valuable, and informative responses that will move your coachee forward far more effectively.

For example, instead of: *"Why did you do that?"*
A more productive question could be: *"What were you hoping to achieve by doing that?"*

Instead of: *"Why didn't you achieve the target?"*
Try: *"What could you do to achieve the target?"*

Instead of: *"Why was this late?"*
Try: *"How could you make sure this is on time in future?"*

Do you get the idea?

The key point to remember is: avoid "Why" questions that lead to negative "because" (justification) type answers that actually disengage your coachee's brain and kill the coaching by leaving you nowhere to go in the conversation.

CHECKLIST

The 7 Types of Questions to Avoid in Your Coaching

❏ Problem-focused questions

❏ Closed questions

❏ Leading questions

❏ Limited choices questions

❏ Irrelevant information gathering questions

❏ Multiple questions

❏ "Why?" Questions

THE 5 INGREDIENTS OF POWERFUL QUESTIONS

Most of us struggle to construct the perfect question and avoid the 7 types of questions that can instantly kill our coaching and waste our time, so I've got 5 ingredients to help you create a powerful question.

This is a quick, simple formula that can help you get powerful results in your coaching – and in your everyday role. You might not have all 5 ingredients in EVERY single question, but you'd certainly have MOST of them in!

Are you ready for the first ingredient?

INGREDIENT 1: Start with a "Whif"! ("What", "How" OR "If")

These are the 3 Magic Words that you MUST begin your question with if you don't want to 'turn off' your coachee. This forces them take a far more active part in the conversation, stops them answering on autopilot, and gets a far better quality, more in-depth and thoughtful response!

Here's a tip for you: Use an "if" question to stop your coachee from focusing on the problem and help them to see past it. If necessary, keep repeating it using 'the broken record technique' and they'll get the message that you expect an answer, so they'll come up with one!

INGREDIENT 2: Add up to 11 words

(To the WHAT, HOW or IF word that you picked for ingredient 1). That keeps it short, simple and clear – especially if you make sure that you avoid acronyms and jargon!

INGREDIENT 3: Copy some of THEIR Language

If your question is in response to something that they've said, don't change their words! Otherwise they could feel that the word they picked in the first place wasn't good enough! Using their words helps build rapport and means that the question is more likely to strike a chord with them.

If you include just these first 3 ingredients, you'll have a really good basic question. Once you've mastered this, you can then go a step further and turn up the heat by adding ingredient 4.

INGREDIENT 4: Substitute "Could" where you can!

This is one of the most IMPORTANT words you can use in your questions. It's really easy...if your question contains words like "would", "should", "do" "will" or "can", simply change it to "could" and you'll instantly encourage more creative thinking!

Notice the difference in how these two sentences sound:

"How CAN you lead your team more effectively?"

"How COULD you lead your team more effectively?"

When we use words like "would", "should", "do" "will" or "can", we're killing creativity. It makes our coachee think that they have to come up with ONE best answer that they "must do" or "ought to do". So what we're going to do as a coach is change it to a "could" to get them to think outside of the box and discover better alternatives and possibilities.

Finally, let's add the icing on the cake wherever we can...

INGREDIENT 5: Add "even"

Look at what difference this makes:

"How could you lead your team more effectively?"

"How could you lead your team EVEN more effectively?"

Notice how adding this one word acknowledges and gives credit for what they're already doing. In fact, you may be aware of companies using this technique when they bring out a 'new and improved' version of their product or service. For example, you've probably seen advertisements for things like: *Even faster broadband, even softer toilet tissue* or perhaps a new phone with *an even better camera.* That way we don't think the previous version was rubbish!

NOW USE THE RECIPE!

So you now know the 5 ingredients of powerful questions. If you follow this recipe and make a conscious effort to master it, you'll soon get even more powerful results in your coaching – and in your everyday role.

Here's a task to help you:

TASK

Pick a lesson or meeting and prepare 3 questions
which contain ingredients 1 <u>AND</u> 2
+ at least 1 of the other ingredients

1. _____

   _____

2. _____

   _____

3. _____

   _____

…Then ask your questions and notice what difference they make!

Finally, once you've asked a powerful question – shut up and give the other person a chance to think, process and respond!

"What is heard in silence can be far more powerful than what can be said with any words."

Katrina Mayer

THINKING TIME — FOR YOU AND THEM!

Pause for a few seconds and think about this – how long do you actually wait after you've asked a question?

'Thinking time' is the amount of time we give after asking a question. Most of us are aware of it, but how many of us actually do it?

If you can add thinking time to your coaching (and to your teaching, meetings or interventions), it will have a huge impact on your coachee's learning, progress and results. So think about your question BEFORE it comes out of your mouth. Remember we're aiming to do 'brain before mouth', so ASK your question and then PAUSE, let them think, and let them answer it. And then, once they've finished answering, wait for at least 3-5 seconds just to check that they've finished BEFORE you ask your next question. That's because they may still be thinking!

It looks and sounds a lot simpler than it is, and that's simply down to the fact that most of us find silence rather uncomfortable, so we tend to jump in and interrupt it. If you do that, you will stop your coachee thinking!

(If you're really uncomfortable, you can always set a time; for example you could say "Spend 30 seconds thinking about this.")

While most of us think we're pretty good at giving thinking time, in actual fact we're not! Research has found that most people typically only wait 0.7 of a second for a response before they jump in! That is simply not long enough!

It's true – if you listen in most classrooms, you'll probably hear this happening. The teacher asks a question, and then rather than waiting, what do they do?

They repeat it, they rephrase it or they answer it themselves!

This is because we often conclude that somebody doesn't know the answer to a question if they don't respond quickly.

It's not true! Nor is it helpful! It actually means that they're thinking, and the fact is: thinking takes time. And with so many questions coming at them, students have virtually zero time to think! As a result, we get the 'autopilot' or 'knowledge' response rather than a deeper thought-through answer which means learning occurs. The bottom line is, the more questions that are asked, the less thinking - and therefore the less learning - occurs.

So don't feel that you're only adding value if you're speaking and asking a lot of questions. In fact, you're better to ask a few powerful questions and then build in thinking time, rather than asking lots of 'knowledge checking questions'. Believe it or not, this simple strategy of shutting up and using 'think time' actually produces significant and profound changes in your coachee. You'll notice things like:

- Increased interest and engagement

- More responses

- Clearer, more in-depth and thoughtful responses

- Better understanding, retention and recall of information

- Better achievement, progress and results

WHAT DOES THIS MEAN FOR YOU?

If you want to become an outstanding coach (and make your teaching, meetings and interventions even better at the same time), you need to make a really conscious effort to avoid all of the things that stop thinking! For example, doing things like:

- Jumping in with another question;

- Interrupting and breaking the silence; and

- Firing question after question after question!

And if you can do that, you'll really take your coaching to the next level and your *Coaching Revolution* will begin to happen.

SUMMARY

Better quality answers come from better quality questions. Avoid the 7 types of questions that can kill your coaching and try to include at least 3 of the 5 ingredients in your questions. Then, once you've asked a powerful question, shut up and give the other person a chance to think, process and respond!

CHAPTER

5

SHUT UP & LISTEN! (CORE SKILL 2)

SHUT UP & LISTEN!

Now that you've developed the core skill of questioning, let's move on to develop the other core skill you need to become absolutely outstanding at - listening - because great coaches are great listeners!

They actually listen for at least 80% of the coaching conversation.

The funny thing is that listening skills are something that most of us tend to take for granted, but in actual fact, most of us often aren't very good at it, because whilst we may hear the sounds, we don't really listen.

Do you know what most people are doing when they're supposed to be listening?

They're attentively waiting for the other person to stop talking so that they can say their bit!

"Most people do not listen with the intent to understand; they listen with the intent to reply."

Stephen Covey

So the danger is that if you were to do this as a coach you'd miss crucial information and the session won't be anywhere near as productive as it could be.

The critical thing to remember is:

No matter how much you're tempted to jump in or give them an idea, if you REALLY want to help someone, you'll need to do something very difficult...

...You'll need to shut up and listen!

And, believe it or not, you'll often learn more by shutting up and listening than by asking questions. That's because listening is far more effective than talking in developing effective working relationships and building your credibility, rapport and trust.

By listening, you'll give your coachees the time and space to work things out for themselves. This will build their confidence, increase their motivation and make them feel far more valued, important and understood. It will also make your coaching more productive because you won't just hear the words; you'll be paying close attention to what they're saying and how they're saying it. By actively listening with your eyes, your ears and your gut, you'll be able to hear beyond the words, understand the real message completely, and then respond in the most effective way. This will enable you to shed light on things for your coachees, or bring things out into the open, which will help them to make much faster progress.

So, in this chapter, you'll learn...

1. The 5 crucial things you need to do to fine-tune your listening

2. What 6 things you need to listen for beneath the surface

3. The 3 responses that will increase your rapport, gain you instant credibility and accelerate your coachee's progress

Just like with questioning, the best way to become really outstanding at this is: work on one aspect at a time, and make a conscious effort to blend it into your everyday role and conversations so that it becomes far more natural and second-nature for you.

HOW TO FINE TUNE YOUR LISTENING

The 5 crucial things you need to do to fine tune your listening are:

1. Eliminate distractions

2. Clear your mind

3. Give your FULL, undivided attention

4. Show them you're listening

5. Use silence

Let's take each one in turn and look at what exactly we need to make a conscious effort to do:

1. **Eliminate distractions** so that you can concentrate fully on the message. Put a sign on the door, turn off your phone and computer screen, and ignore any distracting behaviours, habits or clothes that your coachee might have. In fact, get rid of anything that stops you from giving 100% attention to your coachee, because you can't truly listen to anyone and do anything else at the same time. Distractions will make your coachee feel that you're not really interested in them, and you don't value what they have to say, so your coaching won't be very productive at all!

2. **Take a few minutes to clear your mind** before you coach. The first thing to do is deal with anything that's buzzing around your head – either do it or write it down or set yourself a reminder – especially if you're worried it's something you'll forget later! By the way, if you're on one of our training courses, I'd also recommend that you look at your coaching 'Toolkit', 'Individual Coaching Plan' and 'Log' to remind yourself of the 12-Step Model and questions you'll be asking, and recap your coachee's goal and intended action steps. That will focus you on the conversation you're about to have, so that it's really productive.

3. **Give your FULL undivided attention!** This means stopping what you're doing and keeping an open mind, because otherwise, what we actually hear and what someone actually tells us, can be amazingly different!

Be honest! Do you ever...

...Find your mind wandering to other things or hear your brain 'chattering' away in the background?

...Drift off, especially if somebody goes into lots of details and doesn't really make a clear point?

...Assume some of what they're saying is irrelevant?

...Judge, weigh it up, agree or disagree while they're still talking?

...Anticipate or assume you know what they're going to say or what they are thinking?

...Interrupt people?

...Finish sentences for people?

...Rehearse your response while someone is talking to you?

...Find ideas, suggestions or solutions popping into your head while someone is speaking? If this happens, not only will you miss some of what they're telling you, you'll probably then ask questions that steer them down your path to your best answer. This sets them up for failure because they won't have ownership or 'buy-in'. So block out your ideas and solutions and remember that YOUR best answer isn't necessarily THEIR best answer!

...Chip in with your own story? Perhaps you say something like: *"Oh I know exactly what you mean... I had the same thing happen to me once..."* And then you might even go on to 'top' the speaker's story with one of your stories (which of course is bigger and better than theirs) – so suddenly it becomes all about you! Meanwhile your coachee is left feeling that you're not interested and don't actually really want to know the answer to your question, which can frustrate them, alienate them and shut them down.

These things are fatal to coaching because you won't be paying 100% attention so you could miss crucial information. So if you're doing any of these things, you'll need to make a conscious effort to stop doing them (one-by-one), until you've eliminated them all!

4. **Show them that you're listening:** Stop what you're doing and look at them! Turn towards them, and position yourself at about a 90 degree angle if you can because it's nice and friendly. Try mirroring and matching things like body language, tone and speed. Give them lots of eye contact, lean forward, tilt your head, nod, and every so often say things like, "I see," "I understand," "uh ha," "mmm hmm," and "yes," to show your interest and encourage him or her to continue speaking. Note down 1 or 2 key words so that you're not worrying about rememberingthem. The bottom line is that if you don't make a conscious effort to show your coachee that you're listening, you simply won't get all the information that you need to coach effectively.

5. **Use silence.** This gives them a chance to add anything else they may have thought of, and it gives you time to process the entire message and really 'understand' what they've said (and also what they haven't said!) You can then use the silence to decide what it would be most helpful for you to say next, BEFORE you say it!

Remember to practise these techniques in everyday life. Whenever someone speaks to you, whether it's face-to-face or on the phone, just make a conscious effort to do these 5 things – and notice what a huge difference it makes to the efficiency of the conversation and the quality of information that you get!

"*LISTEN and SILENT are spelled with the same letters – coincidence? I don't think so.*"

Alfred Brendel

LISTEN BENEATH THE SURFACE!

People are often quite guarded when they first begin coaching as they want to protect themselves or preserve the public face that they think other people 'like' and 'approve of.' In other words, they tend to only show us the tip of the iceberg.

Let me ask you something – how much of an iceberg can we see above surface?

It's only about 10%!

So the danger is that if you fail to spot the 90% of the iceberg that's hidden beneath the surface, your coaching could get a serious 'hole' in it that causes it to 'sink'!

An outstanding coach actively listens for what's going on beneath the surface and reads between the lines, so that their coaching is far more powerful and productive. And, as a direct result, they're able to dramatically accelerate their coachee's progress.

So the question is, **what are the 6 critical things that you need to listen for beneath the surface?**

The first thing to listen for is **feelings and emotions**. As a coach, you need to listen past the words and facts. How do they seem to you? What's their tone of voice, facial expressions and body language telling you? Do they seem happy? Sad? Fed up? Excited? Enthusiastic? Upset? Stressed? Distraught? Frightened? Tired? Or perhaps even disappointed?

Next time you speak with someone, try to gauge how they are feeling and ask yourself: *"If I could put a one-word label on how they're feeling, what might it be?"*

So that's the first thing you need to listen for beneath the surface.

The second thing to listen for is **values**. Everyone has values. They're the things that are important to us, so we are naturally drawn towards them because we find them really fulfilling.

Common values are things like: achievement, fun, honesty, loyalty, family, recognition, independence, excellence and education.

The danger is that if you don't listen for your coachee's values it could totally wreck your coaching!

Let me ask you something. Do you know anyone who says that they "want" something, but they just can't seem to make it happen?

That's usually because there's a clash between their goal and their values.

So imagine this – if your coachee set a goal that clashed with his or her values, what's likely to happen?

They won't make much (if any!) progress because they'll lack the energy and enthusiasm to take action. They'll probably also feel frustrated at their own lack of progress and give you lots of 'excuses' (they'll call them 'reasons'!) for why they "couldn't" do it. They'll often say things like: *"I haven't had time!"* or: *"I had to do other things that were far more important!"*

So if you sense a clash between your coachee's goal and their values, you'll need to flag it up for them and get them to modify or re-think their goal so that it's achievable. For instance, you might say something like:

"How could this promotion impact on spending time with your family?"

or: *"How does socialising with your friends fit with passing this exam?"*

Then maybe follow it up with something like: *"What could be a more realistic goal for you?"*

The third thing to listen for is **context**. If you can step into your coachee's shoes and try to see things from their perspective, you'll gain far more information. This can help you build rapport and respond more effectively when you're coaching.

All you need to do is listen out for all the relevant conditions and background circumstances that might be influencing them such as: *what's happened before your meeting, who else is there, what's on their mind, what are their past experiences, or perhaps, what's their agenda?*

Context can also be things like: *how far into the school term it is, what time of day it is, what the weather's like, the furniture, their beliefs, prejudices, fears, concerns, intentions and so on.*

Notice how these sorts of things affect people's energy and motivation levels, how they respond to situations or other people, and even how they speak!

Next time someone is telling you a story, simply ask yourself these 3 questions to understand the context:

• What does the situation look like from their perspective?

• What might be influencing them?

• What's making them respond like that?

So, as you can see, stepping into your coachee's shoes and listening beneath the surface for context is crucial to ensure that you get a much more accurate and complete message.

The fourth thing to listen for is **the will or intention to act**. Try to spot clues that tell you how likely they are to take action. This is crucial because if they're not willing or intending to take action, you're wasting your time coaching them!

The fifth thing to listen for beneath the surface is **what's not being said?** In other words, what are they missing out? What haven't they told you?

This information could be critical to the coaching conversation and will help you to understand the entire message.

The sixth thing to listen for beneath the surface is **what does your inkling or intuition tell you?** In other words – What do you sense or suspect? Make sure you listen to your gut feeling as it's rarely wrong!

So remember, if you listen for these 6 things you'll get beneath the surface, discover a much stronger message, and see the bigger picture, which ultimately means that your coachee will make much better progress.

HOW TO APPLY THIS

When you're confident that you've mastered these listening skills, you'll probably be thinking: *"OK Annie, I've got that. Now what exactly am I going to do with all of this information?"*

Let me show you the 3 responses that will increase your rapport, gain you instant credibility and accelerate your coachee's progress. These are:

1. Asking a relevant question; or

2. Paraphrasing the words, facts or the gist of what they've said; or

3. Reflecting the non-verbal things that you've picked up beneath the surface

Are you ready to have a go?

Look at the following example, and then we'll come up with 3 alternative responses.

Imagine your coachee says:

"I'm so sick of doing everything round here and not getting any support!"

Right, let's break this down. In a nutshell, what's this person saying?

The words are telling us that they feel unsupported, and if we read between the lines they're also saying that they value teamwork, recognition and getting things done and perhaps that other people aren't quite pulling their weight.

Forget the words for a minute - How does the coachee sound to you?

To me they sound quite frustrated, fed up and upset.

So what we're going to do now is use this information to come up with some alternative responses.

As you now know, the first alternative that we've got is to **ask a relevant question:** We can either copy the words (like we did before) – for example we could ask something like, *"How could you get more support?"* – or we could include something 'non-verbal' that we picked up and perhaps ask: *"What could make you feel less frustrated about this?"*

The second thing that we can do is **paraphrasing**. One of the fastest ways to clarify things and show that you've listened and understood somebody is to sum up the key words, facts or gist of what they've said. So in this example we might say something like: *"So you're saying you've got no support at all – is that right?"*

The other advantage of paraphrasing is that it can actually make them re-think the situation and put it into perspective so that they feel better about it, and you get a more accurate picture (and perhaps draw out a little bit more information as well). So in this case they might respond by saying, *"Well actually, no...I wouldn't really say no support..."* and then they could go on to clarify things which could help the rest of your coaching conversation.

The key thing to remember is not to be a parrot and say everything back to them! You are simply showing your coachee that you've listened and understood them by picking out the key points. A really good time to use it is if someone's presented you with a lot of information, or if they seem a bit confused and are doing a lot of waffling.

This simple technique will help you both to see the situation more clearly, encourage more focused discussion and increase your rapport. And this, in turn, results in more growth and faster progress for your coachee. So, if you sense that paraphrasing would be more appropriate than asking a question, you'd pick that one instead.

Your third option is to do some **reflecting**.

People don't just need to feel heard; they need to feel understood. One of the fastest ways to let someone know that you really understand them is to feed back to them what you're sensing from their non-verbal communication (e.g. from their tone of voice, eye contact and posture). This enables you to bring out into the open some of the things that you've heard beneath the surface, which can uncover extra useful information and motivate them to take action.

So in this example you could respond by saying, *"You sound a bit fed up - is that right?"*

The best thing is that you can't really make a mistake with this technique, because even if you get it wrong, they'll immediately tell you the right word. They'll say something like, *"No I'm not fed up, I just feel a bit taken for granted,"* or they'll agree *"Yes. I am fed up about it."*

Either way, your coachee will become much more aware of how they're coming across and they'll feel like you've really listened and understood them. This connection increases your rapport and builds their confidence in themselves and in you as their coach.

YOUR NEXT STEPS

So what do you need to do next?

Practise all of these techniques and make a conscious effort to stop and think: *"What is it most helpful for me to say next?"*

- Is it to ask a relevant question? Is it to paraphrase? Or is it to reflect?

Once you've made your choice: get the response in your head, check it, and then once you're happy with it - say it out loud.

SUMMARY

Aim to listen for at least 80% of the coaching conversation. When you fine-tune your listening you'll build your coachee's confidence and accelerate their progress. Try to listen for the 6 things beneath the surface and then respond in the most effective way by asking a question or paraphrasing or reflecting.

CHAPTER

6

DEVELOPING YOUR MODEL FOR SUCCESS

DEVELOPING YOUR MODEL FOR SUCCESS

Now that you've developed the core skills of questioning and listening, let's move on to think about developing your coaching model. This will give you a framework to structure your coaching conversation so that it's as efficient and productive as possible. You'll simply be asking a series of powerful questions to keep your coachee on track and move them towards their goal. Think of it as a logical step-by-step formula to follow – and then stick to it!

There are hundreds of coaching models out there to choose from, such as: GROW, TGROW, OUTCOMES, COACH, OSKAR, STRIDE, CEDAR and my very own 12-Step Model. You can either save yourself time by picking one of these 'ready-made' models, or you can do what I did and spend years developing your own. (I'll tell you more about that later!)

Of course, like anything new, using a model can feel a bit strange and clunky at first. Don't panic! That's completely normal! You may be tempted to cut corners, jump around or miss steps out – and if you do, you simply won't get the best possible result. Remember – every single step will be there for a reason, and it'll be in that particular sequence for a reason as well. So try to do each step correctly so that your coaching makes maximum impact and your coachee gets maximum benefit. Think of it like learning a new song, and once you've practised it a few times you'll notice that it actually feels incredibly 'natural;' your personality will shine through, and you'll be able to relax and 'make it your own!' (Just stop and think about it for a minute – this is exactly what actors, comedians and TV/radio presenters do – and you know how 'natural' and fluent the best ones sound!)

DO YOU REALLY NEED A COACHING MODEL?

Some people would argue that models are too rigid and constraining. Over the past 18 years I've been lucky enough to work with some of the world's best coaches including Thomas Leonard ("The Father of Coaching"), and I've observed, dissected and experimented with hundreds of coaching approaches. My experience tells me that the most successful coaches all have one thing in common – a clear coaching model which they use consistently in every session.

CONSISTENCY IS KEY!

This really hit home for me recently in my role as an assessor for the *Coaching Quality Mark*. A colleague and I visited a school in The Midlands. Here's what we discovered: The school's Senior Leadership Team was clearly very committed to developing coaching, and all of their coaches were extremely enthusiastic about coaching their colleagues to support them. They'd invested in training from a local university, developed their own coaching model, and assured us that their: *"Staff are coaching all the time, even though they don't always realise it."* It sounded really impressive, so we were quite taken aback with what we found!

What we saw that day was not coaching at all. It was 'professional conversations', 'mentoring' or 'training' with no clear structure or goal.

'Coaches' were making schoolboy errors like leading, advising and suggesting or *telling* the coachee what action steps they should take. Listening time was extremely low (ranging from 31% to 61%) and there were several closed and extremely long questions.

The biggest surprise of all was that their coaching model was not used in any of the 'coaching' sessions that we observed! That was partly down to the fact that some of their coaches had received no training whatsoever in coaching, or the model that they were supposed to be using! (They'd just been given a folder and some proformas). Others knew the model, but they weren't quite certain whether it should be used to structure each individual session or be spread out over a year as a 'long term process'. Believe it or not, their trainers weren't 100% sure either!

So, as you can imagine, coaching in this school made nowhere near as much impact as it could have done if their coaches had been trained by properly qualified experts and given an effective model to use. It's such a shame because despite trying their best, this school had unwittingly put their coaches under unnecessary pressure and potentially set them up for failure. As a result, their coaching sessions lacked effectiveness and took far longer than they needed to. So the moral of the story is...

...A good model will save you lots of time and stress!

It's true! If you're anything like most people who work in schools, you'll be extremely busy, and you'll want an easy, stress-free way to get 'quick wins' and improvements. I'd also imagine you know how frustrating it is when you desperately want to help someone take steps forward, and you're being bombarded with so many challenges or competing priorities that you can't seem to fit everything in.

I've been there, and so have the vast majority of people I've trained. They'd previously been given old, inefficient coaching models (like GROW) to use, which meant that these 'helping conversations' were taking up to an hour of their precious time!

However, once they'd mastered a more powerful model, their coaching conversations became far shorter and far more productive. There was no more 'going round the houses' or time-wasting chit-chat. It was all about getting maximum results with minimum effort so that they had more time to complete the other things on their 'To do' lists.

Pippa Wright is a Senior Teacher at Rosebery School who is completing my online coach training course. In a recent interview, she summed up the huge difference that using my 12-Step Model has made for her:

> *"Using the 12-Step Model has revolutionised my coaching really. Having that 12-Step Model means that you know exactly where you're going to go and how you're going to get there. And you can blitz through something quite quickly because you are following (quite rigidly) that 12-Step Model...It was much quicker and more efficient...It's very focused and you can get very specific goals achieved in a very short space of time."*

Now while most people spend 30-60 minutes coaching, imagine if you could cut this to 15 minutes or less (and make better impact), would that be something you'd find useful?

That's exactly what thousands of our trainee coaches have achieved, and you can easily do it too. It doesn't matter how long you've been coaching or how experienced you are. If you haven't got the right model you won't work as efficiently as you could.

Let me explain...

I first met Kaz in our central Barnsley office, and I was immediately struck by his knowledge, enthusiasm and commitment. Kaz is a highly qualified coach with more than 30 years' experience. As well as working with schools, Kaz coaches busy, high-flying professionals in the city with salaries of £millions (yes you did read that right!) I was really honoured when he decided to come along to my Masterclass because he'd done lots of coaching training before. He'd studied loads of different coaching models, so he soon realised that the 12-Step Model I taught him was completely different and included various elements that he'd never seen in other models. Over the three days, he learnt how to go from around 45 minute sessions to 15 minute sessions, so you can see how much time that's going to save him in the future! Here's what he had to say when one of our brilliant trainers, Jody Kelly, interviewed him. (You may have seen this testimonial on the coachinginschools.com YouTube channel)

"I can see I've learnt absolutely loads in a short space of time...I've been coaching now for probably 30 years in my career, worked in all sectors, and what I would say is, you're never too old to learn. It's definitely been really effective learning, and it's learning how to be really efficient and fast with your coaching and making big results from short spaces of time.

"I thought I knew it, but I didn't know half of it, did I? It's really stretched me, challenged me...but most important, it's been a great learning [experience] for me as well, and great techniques.

"If you're serious about your people, making sure that you get the best out of them, then coaching is the way, and if you want a great model to use, then why not try Annie and coachinginschools.com. It's certainly worked for me, and I'm sure it'll work for you, too."

I felt really moved and humbled by Kaz's words, and that's one of the reasons for this book. Watching his testimonial made me think how many more people I could help if I could get some of these techniques out there! If you implement the things that I've already shown you, and use a good model, you'll be well on your way to success, and I hope, like Kaz, you'll notice how much time this saves you. Sooner or later, you'll also notice the huge difference that this makes to your everyday teaching, leadership and stress level – and to learning, progress and results.

WHY 'OLD' MODELS LIKE 'GROW' SET OFF ALARM BELLS AND DON'T WORK EFFECTIVELY

You're probably familiar with the old, traditional coaching models. They're good for the basics, but the fact is, they don't give you maximum impact. Many people use Sir John Whitmore's GROW model (or variations of it), which is great, and it was a total game-changer for all of us when it was first published back in 1992. Think about it! Just think how much the world has changed since 1992. Back then, there was no Google, no DVDs, no social media; there were hardly any mobile phones, and there was no broadband internet. So as you can see, the world today is radically different. And just like the world has moved on, coaching has moved on, and the 12-Step Model for coaching changes everything because it corrects the things that are 'wrong' with models like GROW, TGROW, OUTCOMES, COACH, OSKAR, STRIDE and CEDAR.

These old models tend to assume that people will set a goal, come up with some options and go away and achieve it. But that's not how people think or operate! They need to break things down and stretch their thinking much more, work around obstacles and leave with a clear, manageable plan with deadlines that they'll be held accountable for.

Here's the thing – the GROW model is easy to teach, but the fact is that it will <u>not</u> get you the best results. Yes, the old models <u>were</u> good back in the day. Now we know they're not as effective as we first perceived them. In fact, they're seriously flawed because they miss steps out, or do them in the wrong order. Therefore, if you're serious about coaching, you'll hear alarm bells ringing in your head and you'll want to stop using them! In fact, that's one reason why a lot of schools fail at coaching – because they're using old models which lack impact and are often taught by non-experts.

Think about it - if you needed a heart operation, you wouldn't go to your mate down the pub that's read one or two books, and ask them to do it, would you? You'd go to a specialist heart surgeon.

It's the same for coaching. You need an expert with a practical working knowledge of coaching in schools, not someone 'cascading back' a diluted version of coaching. I think this Assistant Head summed it up pretty well when he put this comment on his end of course feedback form:

> *"When taught to coach before (on NPQH) it introduced coaching in a whirl, told me that "I can do it", and then let me get on with it as if I was an expert! Your programme forced me to become expert rather than just anointing me so."*

I feel so sorry for people like this. It's not their fault. After all, we can only work with the tools we've got, and many people don't even realise that there are other, better tools out there! It's just a real shame when people are given poor tools in the first place, because they're being set up to fail.

So, I guess the million dollar question for you is:

Do you want to coach?
OR
Do you want to coach well?

If you go ahead and do it the old, slow way then you won't do it well, you won't get maximum benefit, and you won't sustain it, so please think carefully when you select the 'right' coaching model for you and your school. That's exactly what Mark Wright, an Assistant Headteacher from Brentwood County High School did, and in his case study interview he told me:

> *"I only have two experiences – one is the GROW Model, and the other one is Coaching in Schools, and my opinion the Coaching in Schools one completely trumps it!"*

If you'd like to watch the entire Case Study interview I did with Mark, you'll find it here:

www.coachinginschools.com/best-coaching-model-for-schools

HOW MY '12-STEP MODEL' EVOLVED

Now I don't know about you, but I've always set myself high standards. That's why I've personally invested years of my time, and in excess of £100,000 over the last 18 years building my coaching system. I chose to learn 'corporate coaching' from some of the world's best experts when I easily could have done what a lot of people do, and just read a few books or attend a short training event instead. The point is that I don't want to be mediocre; nor do I want any of my coachees or people I train to get mediocre results. That led me on a quest to discover the best coaching model for people in schools.

My goal was to find out what allowed some coachees to make phenomenal progress while others developed a lot more slowly, procrastinated, or failed. I learnt from standing on the shoulders of giants like Thomas Leonard, Sir John Whitmore, Richard Bandler, Jim Collins, Edward de Bono and Ken Blanchard, and then 'joined the dots' between how the brain works and the best practices in teaching and learning, leadership, corporate coaching and Neuro-Linguistic Programming to come up with my own unique coaching system.

I then got people like you involved in testing various coaching models in both state and independent schools, and ensured we included staff and pupils in different areas, ranging from the most deprived to the most affluent – all in an effort to finally get to 'the best model' for ALL schools. I started with basics and then I moved things around. I added bits and I took bits away to see what difference it made. If they were found to improve the coaching process and results achieved, I left them in; if they didn't improve it, I either tweaked them or took them out! I was constantly thinking, "How could I make this even better?" It was a lot of hard work, but I was inspired by the words of Patti Smith who said:

"I would rather write or record something great and have it overlooked than do mediocre work and have it be popular."

The process I used could be summed up as:
Review. Test. Track. Tweak. Repeat.

Having observed, analysed and tracked the impact of thousands of coaching sessions, I finally discovered the model that consistently out-performed ALL others – it was the revolutionary **12-Step Model**.

After that breakthrough, I quickly re-wrote the 'Toolkit' that we give to our trainee coaches so that they could easily follow the steps and get it right. All of our Accredited Trainers now teach this new model so that time-strapped school leaders, teachers and support staff can coach effectively in around 15 minutes (or even less!) So if you want to gain insight into what the best coaches do to make ten times the impact of *'Mr or Mrs Average Coach'*, that's exactly what this model will do for you when you decide to develop your skills further and learn it.

Here are a few brief examples to illustrate the impact that coaches we've trained have achieved by using my 12-Step Model:

- Reducing sickness, absence and the number of staff leaving

- More confidence and effectiveness in leadership, teaching and managing behaviour

- Lower stress levels and improved mental health and well-being for staff and students (stopping them feeling like they were drowning or cracking under pressure)

- Improved engagement and better behaviour for learning (with a lot less conflict and confrontation!)

- Lower truancy rates, improved attendance and punctuality

- Pupils giving more in-depth answers, recalling information more easily in exams, and results going up

- Getting out of 'Special Measures' and going from 'Inadequate' and 'Requires Improvement' to 'Good' and 'Outstanding' *(Ofsted Inspection Ratings)*

- Staff have been coached from **3s** and **4s** to **2s** and **1s** in six weeks or less! (Ofsted Verified)

- All three schools supported by Beauchamp College (a 'National Support School') increased their GCSE Results, going from 37% to 60%; from 40% to 55% and from '20-odd' up to 55%

- Combined reading, writing and maths at Whitefield Primary School went from 37% to 64% in one year and their Ofsted judgement went from 'Requires Improvement' to 'Good'

- A seven year old girl coached by Headteacher Sue Dorban improved her reading by two book band levels within six weeks

- A reception class at Warden Hill Infant School went from just 13.79% to 72.41% of children writing through choice, and also improved their technical writing skills as a result of their teacher being coached for just six 15 minute sessions

- The reading age for a Year 7 boy coached by Sue Yates (Learning Resource Centre Manager) increased by 1 year and 7 months in six weeks

- 63.64% of C/D borderline students at St Bernard's Catholic High School who were coached achieved C grades in their Science GCSE compared with just 33.33% of students who were mentored

- Increase in 'value added' and 'Progress 8' scores

- Better progress and attainment *(e.g. English grades boosted from a 'D' to an 'A', Maths GCSE grade boosted from a 'D' to a 'B', a pupil who was refusing to put pen to paper was coached* *from a U to a B grade, Science coursework grades went from Ds and Es to Bs and A*s, a pupil's SATS level increased from 4a to 6b, and thirteen Year 5 under-achieving pupils doubled their rate of progress to achieve their age-related targets (or above) and their end of year targets)*

I don't know if you can relate to any of these examples, but I find it amazing and humbling to see people get such incredible results so quickly having worked with us and learnt our coaching system.

In fact, every time I talk to our trainee coaches, I hear moving and incredible stories that inspire and surprise me, like the fact that all trained coaches at Beauchamp College have been promoted. And it's not just stories about the difference it's made to their professional lives; it's the impact on their personal lives as well.

I'll never forget one presentation where the trainee put up a PowerPoint slide which showed a photo of a young woman who was dressed up to go out, complete with a bottle of wine in her hand. With tears in her eyes this coach said: *"This picture won't mean much to any of you, but it means the world to me. This is my daughter, and before coaching, she was in a serious depression. She couldn't even get out of bed in the morning and wouldn't go out anywhere. I was desperately worried about her, and I didn't know how to help her. Other things hadn't worked, so I tried coaching on her. She's now able to get out of bed, and this photo shows her going out for the evening for the first time."*

Another trainee coach told of how she'd used coaching to help a friend in the Muslim community to escape dreadful domestic violence which she'd been suffering for years.

And Year 11 student, Danielle John, told me that coaching had stopped her from cracking under exam pressure and having a mental breakdown. Before she was coached she felt:

> "Stressed is one word! I was absolutely terrified of walking into the exam hall. I had to do my exam in a different room…I was overwhelmed. There was so much to do. There was so much work in each subject to do. And all of the teachers were expecting you to know everything with each subject, and there were just too many subjects to know, so I was just overwhelmed. And you know when you look at a problem and you just think 'Oh, that's too big, I'm not even going to bother with it?' – That's what I was like."

After just 6 short coaching sessions (using the 12-step model), Danielle was able to enter the exam hall confidently, and she found it much easier to recall the information she needed for answering her exam questions.

As a result of being coached she felt:

> "Like a weight's been lifted off my shoulders. It sounds so cliché, I know, but it really does. It's crazy how weird it feels. Like the fact that before, you have the stress and it's like…it feels like a literal weight on your shoulders. And then afterwards, it's like 'Whoa! OK! Wow! I've just finished that whole chunk of stuff that I needed to do, and now I feel like a whole space in my brain has been cleared for new information.' And it's actually so great it's made me happier as a person, and it made me a kinder person, because I was kind of moody all the time (because I was just stressed)…It really does have an impact on your persona and your character. It just makes you a better person, I think."

In light of her own coaching experience, Danielle feels that all pupils could benefit academically and emotionally from being coached, and her message to Headteachers worldwide is:

"You need to learn how to do that! Because having that skill and being able to change…because Ms Austin's changed my life. That sounds so cliché again, but honestly she has. And I feel like if more people had the training and the expertise to do that to other people, then it would just be so fantastic - because I'm just one person that she's helped. There could be so many more people that could feel the way that I feel now and that would just be like a magic power. Honestly it would be like a superpower!"

If you'd like to watch the video of Danielle's case study, you'll find it at:

www.coachinginschools.com/coaching-pupils

As I'm listening to stories like this, I find myself sitting there with my jaw on the floor and tears rolling down my cheeks, and I'm thinking, *"Wow! - This is really powerful stuff!"*

I could never have predicted that my coaching system would help so many people in so many different ways. I find it really amazing, but I'm not taking any credit here. Yes, I was the creator, but of course these trainees have to take the credit themselves, because they're the ones that actually go and do it for real when we ask them to put their learning into practice. I was just the facilitator, and I'm delighted that so many people are getting such great results and making so much impact (both inside and outside of school) by using my 12-Step Model, the techniques, the tools, the support, and everything else that makes up the 'magic formula' in my Best I.M.P.A.C.T. Blueprint®

I'll explain it more in Chapter 7, but in a nutshell, this blueprint gives you a step-by-step roadmap which enables your school to become 'self-improving'. And, of course, it also means that you don't have to have that same long journey I had, because you can choose to leverage my skills and experience so that you can get better results, just like these colleagues who now have skills that they can use for life!

Mark Wright, the Coaching Project Manager at Brentwood County High School summed it up perfectly when he said:

> *"It really empowers and enables the people being coached to come up with solutions to any problem in any walk of their life, whether it's problems with finances, problems at home or problems at work – but in a way that is totally facilitated by the coach through those 12 steps and those 'what', 'how' and 'if' questions. We've had some sceptics do the course over these last two years and they have been totally converted by their experiences. It isn't only a valuable tool to use in your working life – it's an amazing tool to use in your own personal life and every walk of life. Anything that requires a solution – that is the way to do it! – And I think that anyone who trains with Coaching in Schools to get this is developing skills for life."*

By the way, if you're thinking to yourself that you'd like to get started straight away, you can learn the 12-Step Model right now when you enrol in my online training course [**www.training.coachinginschools.com**] where I'll personally guide you through it step-by-step.

As I said in the introduction, much as I'd love to, I can't teach you the 12-Step Model in this book because it would be a bit like me saying: *"Spend 10 minutes reading this helicopter pilot's manual, then jump in with your best mate, fire it up, and fly it as far and as fast as you can in the next 15 minutes!"*

You'd probably end up seriously injuring yourself or your friend, so it would be pretty reckless of me to suggest it, wouldn't it?

It's the same with coaching. Often when you're doing new things on your own, you can accidentally get it wrong and cause damage to other people.

It's also easy to lose motivation, or lose faith in the process, just because of a lack of experience, since you'll be making a lot of mistakes that you probably won't be aware of. And, even if you are aware of them, you probably won't know how to put those mistakes right. So you really need someone to hold your hand, guide you through, answer your questions (as and when they come up), and hold you accountable for taking action.

If you talk to any of our trainee coaches or Accredited Trainers, they'll tell you that these mistakes (and corrections) happen all the time at our coaching skills assessments, and that's why we build them into our programmes at an early stage. It means we can highlight each individual coach's key strengths and give them constructive tips so that they know exactly how to take their coaching to the next level. Most importantly, we want to pick up any 'bad' habits before they become ingrained!

Can you imagine what could happen otherwise?!

SUMMARY

If you want the best possible results from coaching you need a powerful up-to-date model like my 12-Step Model which is fast and efficient, NOT an 'old' inefficient model (like GROW, TGROW, OUTCOMES, COACH, OSKAR, STRIDE or CEDAR). You can either do what I did, and spend the next 18 years developing your own model from scratch, or you can leverage my skills & experience and take the short-cut for faster results!

... It's up to you!

If you want to accelerate your learning and get started with the programme right now, please go to:

www.training.coachinginschools.com

If you have any questions about the programme, or if you would like to speak to me directly, please email me at annie@coachinginschools.com

CHAPTER

7

QUICK WINS FOR INSTANT SUCCESS WHEN COACHING

SHORTCUT YOUR SUCCESS

Let me ask you something…

…What's the point of reinventing the wheel when you can take what's worked for the most successful coaches and apply it directly to your coaching?

With anything in life, you can do it the long, hard way, or you can do it the short, easy way. And I think most of us would rather do it the short way – the easy way – and save ourselves a lot of time, a lot of hassle, and a lot of money. So, in this final chapter, I'll be sharing with you 10 simple yet powerful 'quick wins' which will increase your efficiency and effectiveness as a coach and/or coaching project manager.

Ready?

QUICK WIN #1:
TAKE PART IN THE #COACHINGCHALLENGE

One of the fastest ways to get quick wins in your coaching is to take part in the weekly #coachingchallenge. It's a free resource which is posted on Twitter and Facebook at 8:30pm every Sunday (except during the summer holidays), and it's completely free to join in.

You'll find it's a fast, fun and easy way to hone your skills, because you'll be integrating coaching principles into your everyday life and work, and as a result, they'll start to become second-nature for you. Your learning will then naturally transfer into your coaching sessions, and your coaching will become far more efficient and effective.

How to join in:

- Follow @schoolcoachguru on Twitter
  [www.twitter.com/schoolcoachguru]

- Search 'coaching in schools' on Facebook and 'Like' the page
  [www.facebook.com/coachinginschools]

QUICK WIN #2:
STICK TO A REGULAR TIME SLOT

I know it sounds ridiculous, but imagine if a TV channel kept chopping and changing the day and time of your favourite programme – or if your fitness training was at 9am one week, 11am the next week, and 7:30pm the week after – it would be hard to keep up with it, wouldn't it?

You'd probably lose track, lose interest and possibly even stop engaging with it altogether.

It's the same with coaching – those people who book in regular time slots tend to be more successful than those people who don't, so agree a regular time slot with your coachee on week 1 to make your coaching instantly more successful.

QUICK WIN #3:
POINT TO THE GOAL

Believe it or not, many coaches get so caught up in the coaching that they forget the coachee's goal! As a result, the session isn't anywhere near as effective as it should be.

A quick and easy way to avoid this is by having your coachee's coaching plan and log in front of you. This will help keep you and your coachee focused on both their end of cycle target and their goal for the session. You can then simply point to it or refer back to it to stop any time-wasting tangents!

QUICK WIN #4:
STICK TO THE MODEL!

What's the point of having a system if you don't follow it properly?

During our practical skills assessments, we often find inexperienced coaches jumping around the model, doing steps in the wrong order, missing steps out or changing the questions into closed or long-winded ones (without even realising it!)

As you can imagine, this dramatically reduces their efficiency and effectiveness, so make sure that you don't do that! Just stick to the model and you can't go far wrong!

By the way, don't put yourself under pressure to learn it off by heart. All you need to do is glance down at the next step and see what it says, then look up, make eye contact and say it! Then, as you get more confident and experienced, you can gradually build in the more advanced coaching skills like the 7 secrets that you'll learn when you're on our training.

QUICK WIN #5: DON'T BE A NARRATOR!

When you first start coaching, it's tempting to narrate or explain the model as you go.

This is completely unnecessary and time-wasting.

Your coachee doesn't need to know the process; they need to be able to think! And if you narrate the process, you'll actually reduce the effectiveness of your coaching, and sessions will take you a lot longer.

So instead of doing this, make sure you do what the most successful coaches do, and simply ask the next question!

QUICK WIN #6: FILL IN THE 'PAPERWORK' AS YOU GO

Whilst there's hardly any paperwork to do, some coaches waste valuable time by making unnecessary, copious notes during sessions, when they actually only need to jot down one or two words (if anything!) Other coaches duplicate notes by writing information on the wrong document during the session, and then copying it up on the correct document afterwards!

The most successful coaches record the key information needed, succinctly on the correct paperwork as they go, so make sure you do that too! *(By the way, a great tip for those of you who are working with our 'Toolkit' is to read the 'Quick Start Guide' on page 1 and pay particular attention to 'the key' so you don't become a human photocopier!)*

QUICK WIN #7:
ASK THEM TO SUM UP ANY WAFFLE!

This is one of my favourite quick wins! Over the years I've had several emails and phone calls from trainee coaches saying:

"Hi Annie, one of my coachees talks too much!
They go on and on, and I get a bit lost and sessions take ages.
- Help! What can I do?"

Does that sound familiar?

If so, here's a great tip for you – if your coachee is waffling, (or goes off at a tangent), simply ask them: "How could you sum that up in one sentence?" or: "How could you sum that up in one or two words?"

That's a powerful technique to get them back on track, and it also crystallises their thoughts for both of you.

QUICK WIN #8:
SET A TIMER

If you're into productivity, you'll know that Parkinson's Law states that *'work expands to fill the time available for its completion.'* So this means that if you give yourself 'leg room' of say an hour to complete a 15 minute coaching session, then (psychologically speaking), the coaching is highly likely to take you much longer than 15 minutes, and probably fill the best part of that hour!

It's funny, because people often don't become fully aware of how quickly coaching can be completed until they test this principle out.

We do this in our practical coaching skills assessments, by having a countdown timer running in the background. And because our trainees know the timer is running, guess what happens?

Well, as you'll see for yourself in the 'fly-on-the-wall' live recordings that are part of our training resources, 99% of people easily complete their coaching (without rushing) within the 15 minutes given!

The great news is that you can easily do the same to improve your efficiency – simply set yourself a timer!

QUICK WIN #9:
FOLLOW UP AND HOLD THEM ACCOUNTABLE!

Surprisingly, a lot of coaching 'slips' because coaches forget to follow up, and hold their coachee accountable!

Be honest! If at the end of this book you said to me, *"Annie, here's what I'm going to do…"* (and then gave me a list of all your action steps) – Hand on heart, would you DEFINITELY do absolutely <u>everything</u> that was on your list?

Most people wouldn't.

What if you knew I was going to be checking up on you – would you be more likely to do it then?

Most people would!

Now imagine I'm coaching you, and at the end of our session, I pick up my phone, then turn to look you and casually say, *"I'm just going to pop that in my diary so I remember you'll be emailing me at 4pm on Thursday."*

You then watch me enter the reminder and save it.

How would that make you feel?

If you're anything like most people, your response will be:

"I've REALLY got to do it!"

So, as you can see, this is a brilliant way keep your coachee on track. You just need to remember:

1. Don't micromanage – it's best to group action-steps together into check-ins.

2. Make check-ins easy (e.g. they could cc or bcc you into an email they were sending anyway, as part of their action plan).

3. Follow up to hold them accountable if they *don't* check in with you as agreed!

QUICK WIN #10: USE THE 'BEST I.M.P.A.C.T. BLUEPRINT'® AS YOUR ROADMAP

In the case study which follows this chapter, you'll see how outstanding Headteacher Monica Austin created an effective coaching culture in her school – and you can easily follow this roadmap to do the same.

In fact, you might also want to bookmark this page now, and share this 'quick win' with your Headteacher to get their buy-in, because they're obviously responsible for setting the strategic direction of the school.

Not only will this blueprint help them to easily write coaching into your School Improvement Plan and SEF, it'll also help to develop their vision and show them that they're investing in something which is valuable and sustainable.

So what exactly is the 'Best IMPACT Blueprint'®?

In a nutshell, it's a logical strategic action plan (and checklist) which I've developed for schools who want to introduce and embed coaching effectively. It gives them the EXACT roadmap to do it, so all they need to do is follow it (step-by-step) and tick it off as they go. This stops them from accidentally taking a wrong turn or going the long, inefficient way (which is what most schools do!)

Here's a brief overview so that you can see how it works:

When you begin your journey, you'll be invited to pick from a range of training solutions, so make sure you pick the one which best meets your needs, works around your constraints and delivers your intended outcomes. You'll then need to invite and select the right people to be trained. Whatever you do, don't just accept anyone! They need to be right for it, and it needs to be right for them! *(That's why people aren't automatically accepted onto our courses – they have to meet our "3Rs Criteria" for their application to be approved).*

M   MASTER

Once accepted, your coaches undertake the journey to master the different modules of the Coaching System, which means they'll become true instigators of change. To achieve this quickly and easily, you obviously need to make sure your coaches are trained by genuine experts, given specialist support, and 100% relevant resources which are specifically designed for busy people in schools.

That's exactly why Salford City Academy approached me. In her case study interview, Carol Murray who led the programme told me:

> *"We wanted an expert to come in and guide us, because what we didn't want to do was do things wrong and cause detrimental effect with the staff. We didn't want it to go backwards, obviously! We didn't want to do a trial and error where again, things could go drastically wrong, and it would actually not do what we wanted it to do...*

"The impact of that has been tremendous. We targeted the staff who really needed support straight away. Within a six-week programme, staff who were achieving grade 4 'unsatisfactory' lessons were turning that around very, very quickly.

*"Ofsted targeted members of staff who had actually **drastically** improved, because they were seeing that this person was a grade 4, and then suddenly we've said that they're a 2. So they observed a number of our teachers who were being challenged, and their grades from the Ofsted inspection observations were again 2s and frequently were 1s.*

"None of our teachers who'd been on the coaching package got anything less than a 2."

If you'd like to watch Carol's Case Study interview, you'll find it here:
www.coachinginschools.com/coaching-teachers

P | PRACTISE

We all know we need to do something regularly or repeatedly to become skilled at it, so if you want to become an outstanding coach, you'll want to practise your core skills, your advanced skills (like the 7 secrets) and, of course, your coaching conversations. The danger at this stage of the journey is that if you rely on 'goodwill' you'll slow down the process, and risk it 'fizzling out'.

To avoid this, you need to make coaching manageable so that it's not an 'add-on' and doesn't take any extra time. At coachinginschools.com we use something I call *"The I.C.E. Principle,"* to help coaches easily incorporate it into their everyday roles, so that new techniques become truly embedded.

However, whilst it's often said that 'practice makes perfect' – I disagree.

You could actually be reinforcing bad habits!

The smart way is to have an expert observing your practice and giving you personalised feedback on real (LIVE) coaching sessions. When you practise in this way, you'll know EXACTLY how to improve the quality and efficiency of your coaching, so you'll be able to make even more impact on the quality of teaching, learning and leadership.

A | ANALYSE

Once you've mastered the basics of coaching and practised until you're proficient, your next stage in the journey is to use 2 powerful diagnostic tools to support your school's self-evaluation, team evaluation, and peer evaluation. These comprise:

1. Giving Feedback 'Coach-Style' on 7 Key Features

2. A 'dual factor' 360° Feedback School Improvement (SI) and School Self-Evaluation (SSE) tool [www.360feedbackinschools.com]

When you add these tools to your coaching 'Toolkit,' you'll save yourself a lot of time and money, because they'll show you what's working well for your coachee(s) and what exactly they need to work on to take their performance to the next level.

The 360 tool will also automatically pinpoint specific 'strengths', 'development areas', 'hidden strengths' and 'blind-spots' for you. It then forensically analyses data for individuals, teams or your whole school to:

a) Match up your 'experts' with people who are performing 'below expectations'

AND

b) Show you the top three improvement priories so you can be 100% certain that you're focusing on the most important aspects of their performance to improve.

Not only does this mean that your coaching (and Continuing Professional Development) can be far more personalised, relevant and effective, but you'll also be able to provide far more effective peer-to-peer and school-to-school support.

You can then track progress, measure the impact of your coaching and hold your coachees to account more easily! As a result, you'll be able to eliminate under-performance, say goodbye to frustrating inconsistent practice and 'excuses', and raise standards more rapidly across your school.

C CONSOLIDATE

The coaching approach needs to be consolidated and embedded into your school to make it sustainable. We use something called 'The L.E.A.P.S. Formula,' which is a simple system that helps you join the dots to develop a true coaching culture and ensure that coaching takes place as planned.

Getting this right means that it's perceived as a positive (not remedial) approach, and with Senior Leadership support, you'll be able to increase the scope and potential of coaching for staff and pupils at all levels, and permeate the coaching ethos throughout your school.

You can then gain recognition for this with the Coaching Quality Mark [www.coachingqualitymark.co.uk]

When the demand for coaching increases (or your trained coaches leave), you'll need to think about building your coaching capacity.

Even with the best will in the world, your coaches probably haven't got time to take on a massive caseload!

So, what are your options?

Well, it'll obviously depend on the provider you're working with, but to give you an idea, if you were working with us, you could ask us to train more coaches for you. Alternatively, we can train your best coaches to train others as part of a licensing agreement.

If you're serious about developing coaching, this is the most cost-effective and sustainable way to roll out coaching in your school over a few years. It also gives you an opportunity to generate income for your school, if that's something you'd find useful.

So, when you get to this final stage of the journey, make sure you plan your next steps for training others, then simply follow the Best IMPACT Blueprint® journey again with your new cohort of trainee coaches.

'MARGINAL GAINS'

It's easy to underestimate the value of these 'quick wins', but when you make a conscious effort to implement them, you'll gradually improve your coaching. Whilst you might not notice the improvements at first, if you keep implementing these 'quick wins' consistently, they'll add up to remarkable improvements in the efficiency and effectiveness of your coaching and the way you work.

This is the concept of 'marginal gains'. It's revolutionised sports, businesses and healthcare, and you can easily apply this approach to improve both your coaching and your school's outcomes.

In fact, this is the exact method adopted by the legendary British Cycling performance director, Sir Dave Brailsford. The British Cycling Team went from winning just one gold medal in 76 years, to winning eight gold medals at the 2008 Beijing Olympic Games – a remarkable achievement! He then used the same principle to lead Team Sky to victory in the 2012 Tour de France, just two and a half years after he took over.

Sir Dave achieved this by breaking down everything that could impact on a cyclist's performance and aiming to improve it by just 1%. This resulted in the team making tiny incremental improvements in lots of different areas, which added up to a huge increase in their overall performance and outcomes. And it'll be exactly the same for you when you apply this principle in your coaching and in your everyday role.

Imagine if each of these 'quick wins' improved your coaching by just 1%. What difference could that make overall?

"You can achieve optimal performance by the aggregation of marginal gains."

Sir Dave Brailsford

STOP AND THINK!

As you've stuck with me this far, I'm guessing you're serious about making your coaching as powerful as possible. Therefore, I'd recommend that you take a few minutes to stop and think about the common mistakes schools make when developing 'coaching'.

After analysing and picking up the pieces of hundreds of 'failed' coaching programmes in schools over the past 18 years, I've noticed that there are several recurring things that come up over and over again that contribute to the success (or failure) of coaching in the education sector. In fact, there are 10 particular mistakes that my trainers and I come across a LOT!

In addition to being motivated and incredibly passionate about helping their colleagues and pupils to overcome their biggest challenges, there are multiple 'fool-proof' strategies that the most successful coaches in schools have used to avoid these mistakes and make a huge impact every single day.

If you'd like to shortcut your success and make sure that you can avoid the pitfalls too, I'd urge you to take advantage of the special bonus gift that I've put together for you. It's a comprehensive report called 'The 10 Common Mistakes Schools Make When Developing Coaching – And How To Avoid Them!' (We sell it at £7 but I want to give it to you completely free of charge, to thank you for reading my book).

If you haven't done so already, you can download it immediately, by registering your details at:

www.coachinginschools.com/book-offer

Last, but by no means least, as we're approaching the end of this book, I guess the million dollar question is…

...WHAT ARE YOU GOING TO DO NOW?

Having read this book, you've now got a good level of knowledge to go out there and make a difference to the people you work with. Obviously, this isn't the end of the road. It's actually the beginning of your journey, and I feel incredibly grateful and privileged to have been part of it.

Everything we've covered in this book will give you a solid foundation to get started with this new, clever way of coaching. You've got some great tools, techniques and 'quick wins' to help you in your coaching (and in your everyday role), so the key is to turn that knowledge into action.

It's easy to do, but it's also very easy not to do!

Whilst everyone who's read this book COULD do it, some simply won't. They'll keep putting it off, they'll make excuses, and they'll tell themselves stories about why others can do it and why they can't, or why the time isn't right.

In actual fact, everyone can do it (if they choose to), and the time is ALWAYS right because this strategy has no sell-by date and it will have more impact than anything else on EVERY aspect of school improvement.

So the question is: **What exactly are you going to do now?**

As you know, the number 1 reason most people fail is because they don't take action, but as you've got to the end of this book, I have faith that you're one of the 'doers', and not just one of the 'talkers'! I guarantee if you follow the concepts, strategies, and 'Best Impact Blueprint'® in this book correctly, you'll be rewarded with a wonderful sense of fulfilment as you help to change the careers, lives and futures of a vast number of people.

I hope you've enjoyed this book and got value from it. I also hope you're now feeling that you'd like to start your own *Coaching Revolution*. If you'd like my help, advice and more training, so that you can secure even more powerful results, then please email me at:

annie@coachinginschools.com

or give me a ring on **+44 (0)1636 351 352**

Whatever you decide, good luck with it all, and keep me posted with how you get on. I can't wait to hear about your successes!

Annie

SUMMARY

If you're serious about becoming an outstanding coach you'll want to implement these 'quick wins' and develop your coaching skills further so that you can increase your efficiency and effectiveness. When you decide to continue your journey by taking action and getting support from an expert you'll be able to make even more impact as a coach and your school will benefit from even better teaching, leadership and outcomes. You can either continue your journey now, or you can put it off and regret it. It's up to you.

*"A year from now you may wish
you had started today"*

Karen Lamb

CASE STUDY

ASHCROFT HIGH SCHOOL

By Monica Austin
Headteacher

I'M PASSIONATE ABOUT COACHING!

I was first introduced to the concept while completing various NCSL courses. I loved coaching's potential for empowering staff and facilitating personal and professional growth. I recognised the limits of mentoring; telling people what to do and how to do it has an important role in passing on professional expertise, but it isn't the correct vehicle for training staff to resolve their own challenges.

Back in 2011 the school had emerged from the ashes of 'special measures' to be judged as 'outstanding' overall, but not in all areas of provision. I knew that coaching was the perfect vehicle for securing ongoing improvements. And yet coaching wasn't happening across the school!

Why not?

For several reasons:

- We'd already had a formal coaching structure in place that had involved all staff. It became so complex and unwieldy that it collapsed!

- Our coaching model had relied heavily on staff goodwill, as it had been difficult to find time for the one hour coaching sessions in the school day.

- Our coaches weren't trained. We paired people up and said *'go forth and coach!'* with no clear direction. I dread to think what the quality of those coaching conversations was like!

- Despite my NCSL coaching courses I wouldn't have been able to train anyone to be an effective coach…because I couldn't actually remember any of the courses I'd participated in! I vaguely remembered the skills they focussed on, such as listening skills, but there was no clear structure for using those skills.

In a nutshell, coaching wasn't happening at Ashcroft because I wasn't prepared to repeat my mistakes of the past. Coaching is such a powerful strategy for staff development that I knew I had to get it right before re-introducing it across the school.

WHY COACHINGINSCHOOLS.COM?

My deputy, Julie Clarke, attended an 'Introduction to Coaching in Schools' run by the company's Managing Director and trainer, Annie Boate. Julie came back waxing lyrical about Annie and about the coaching programme. She understood the school's improvement priorities and was adamant that Annie's coaching programme was exactly what we needed.

I trust Julie 100%. If she says something will have impact across the school, then I know it will. 100%!

And yet I hesitated.

Strategically I still hadn't worked out how to make the coaching work across the school. I couldn't afford to get it wrong a second time. So I held off giving Julie the go-ahead. But you haven't met Julie! 'Tenacious' is her middle name! She was so convinced that we needed Annie and her coaching programme, that she refused to give up badgering me. She refused to let me forget about her proposal.

Eventually I came up with a strategic plan that might work!

I would try out Annie's coaching programme on the 12 members of our core and extended SLT. We would be cohort 1 and we could fit our coaching sessions into our scheduled line management sessions. And if Julie had got it wrong for the first time since I'd known her, I'd simply say 'thank you and farewell' to Annie Boate after cohort 1, and bury the course!

THE 'COACHING JOURNEY' FOR COHORT 1 (SLT)

So at Ashcroft we began our coaching journey with Annie in December 2012. The first thing that struck me before the course even started was Annie's organisation, efficiency and professionalism. The course programme was clearly communicated, we knew exactly what we needed to provide for each session as a school, and each participant received a comprehensive welcome email with joining instructions. Annie was there at least an hour early before each session to check materials and deal with any last-minute glitches from the school end.

From the first moment of the first session with Annie, we were all fully engaged, thanks to her lively presentation skills and her outstanding subject knowledge. She has a wonderful way of challenging you and taking you out of your comfort zone while at the same time making you believe you can do it.

During the 8 training sessions, she constantly challenged our assumptions about our core coaching skills. For example, we all thought we were fantastic listeners until, 10 minutes into Annie's session on listening skills, we all changed our minds when we saw our dreadful scores on the listening test she set us! She then taught us how to make our listening 'even better,' and by the end of the session, our collective despair had turned to hope, and we were keen to get out there and practise our new skills.

I have to confess that I was personally terrified of making a fool of myself on the course. After all, as the Headteacher, I'm meant to be omniscient, and a constant role-model, whether awake or asleep (or so I've been told!). And yet there was so much I was discovering that I didn't know. And Annie's extremely high standards meant that none of us were allowed to get away with anything less than our best efforts, whoever we were!

By the second session, I lost my fear and began to appreciate the unique opportunity for growth. As members of SLT, we were all participating in the same learning experience with an equal chance of success. This created an additional bond between us as a team that impacted positively on our everyday working relationships.

My most important discovery during the training lies at the very heart of Annie's coaching system.

I call it 'the missing link.'

I finally realised why I had so quickly forgotten all my previous coaching courses. None of them had provided me with a model for structuring my coaching conversations. I had nothing concrete to hang my disparate coaching skills on. Annie provided this missing element by teaching us her 12-Step Model. During each coaching conversation, the coach moves through the same 12 steps in the same order. There's not even a need to learn the 12 steps by heart – the coaching toolkit provided by Annie acts as a guide for each conversation.

I couldn't believe how time-efficient the 12-Step Model was; coaching conversations were taking 15 minutes instead of the hour that we had assigned to them in our previous whole-school coaching system. How much precious time we had wasted! The coachinginschools.com model was fast, efficient and effective.

Neither could I believe the impact the coachinginschools model was having. As trainee coaches, we all experienced coaching others and being coached ourselves. The goals we set ourselves in our practice coaching sessions were all real-life challenges we were facing at that time.

As coachees, the structure of the 12-Step Model and being held to account by the coach led to us making real progress with the issues we had identified, and with the solutions we had come up with for ourselves. As coaches, it was gratifying to see, feel and hear our coachees' relief as they made incremental progress in solving a problem that had been keeping them awake at night.

The monthly training sessions with Annie were a perfect way of absorbing a lot of new information in an accessible way. It also gave us the time to practise, practise, practise our new coaching skills in-between sessions.

I loved the non-hierarchical structure of the coachinginschools model. All coaches use the same 12-Step Model, so anyone can be coached by anyone. My business manager coaches me. My deputy coaches me. And one of the maths teachers who has completed the course will soon begin coaching me.

I've used my sessions as a coachee to produce key school improvement and self-evaluation tools.

We also appreciated the ongoing support that we received from Annie in between sessions. As we began our coaching journey, we came up against challenges and questions that needed immediate clarification.

It's so easy to embed poor practice through lack of good feedback. Annie was always accessible via email and her rapid responses always put us back on the right track.

What amazed me more than anything was the impact that the coaching training was having on so many areas of school life.

It was changing our mindset and our language as participants. We thought more about the impact of our words. It improved our questioning skills with staff, parents and in lessons. We listened to others more actively and more effectively. We inter-wove parts of the 12-Step Model into our everyday conversations to good effect. Our conversations with staff became more solution-focussed and more time-efficient.

It became clear to me after the first session with Annie that Mrs Clarke had proved her worth yet again! Instead of 'burying' the coachinginschools system, I realised that I needed to spread the 'coaching revolution' across the school that had tentatively started with cohort 1.

ASHCROFT'S COACHING REVOLUTION

Ashcroft needed the coachinginschools.com system as our primary vehicle for staff development. Following the success of cohort 1, my strategic plan was to get Annie to train the following staff as accredited coaches:

Cohort 2: all leaders with line management responsibilities, to include new SLT and middle leaders

Cohort 3: all teaching staff with departmental development responsibilities, to include key stage and intervention co-ordinators

Cohort 4: all support staff with pastoral responsibilities. I was keen for our students to experience the benefits of being coached. All support staff with line management responsibilities, including admin staff

The coaching revolution has now spread throughout the school, and Annie is preparing to train cohort 5 as I write this.

'Coaching envy' is now rife at Ashcroft, with staff approaching me to find out when they are going to get the chance to be trained as an accredited coach. This is because they have experienced the power of being coached, so they are eager to learn the skills for themselves.

The final strand of my strategy is to be accredited as a coaching school via the Coaching Quality Mark within the next year.

WHAT WAS THE PROBLEM WITH MY STRATEGY?

There was only one problem with my carefully-crafted coaching strategy back in 2013. Once I had experienced for myself the significant impact of Annie's course, I realised that I couldn't wait for all staff to become accredited coaches cohort by cohort. There was a more immediate need for all staff to share a common coaching language and approach in their everyday work at Ashcroft. I needed the coaching approach to permeate Ashcroft and become 'the Ashcroft way.'

Consequently, I commissioned Annie to run 1 hour sessions for all teaching and support staff as an introduction to 'The Coaching Approach'. These sessions covered the basic ingredients of coaching and effective questioning.

WHAT WAS THE IMPACT?

The impact across the school was immediate; all staff were able to improve their questioning techniques without delay – not just the ones who were lucky enough to be on Annie's coaching course. Teachers improved their questioning in lessons; staff improved their interactions with students around the school; interviews with parents improved; line management conversations were better structured, and so the list of benefits went on.

I began to see the relevance of the coaching approach in so many unexpected and seemingly 'unconnected' areas of our work. For example, my new coaching skills made me dissatisfied with the way we interviewed staff and the questions we asked. When I reviewed our interview questions, I was embarrassed by the number of 'closed' questions included.

Appointing the right staff in a school is so crucial, and yet our interview methods are often archaic and a bit of a hit-and-miss affair! I thought of how genuine, honest and productive our coaching conversations were. I wanted to reproduce those same outcomes in our staff interviews.

I now use the coaching approach to plan effective interview questions and I've changed the format of the final interview with candidates. This is now much more like a coaching conversation; the setting is relaxed, with the candidate doing 80% of the talking, having been asked very open questions that invite them to respond with honesty.

The result is that the person we see and hear tends to be the genuine version, rather than the one that's been crafted to pass interviews. It's a lot easier to select the right candidate for the school when you're interacting with the real person you'll be working with on a daily basis!

Annie's coaching programme includes a module on giving feedback 'coach-style'. All feedback following lesson observations is now based on the methodology from this module. The teacher is invited to identify their own improvement priority following the lesson (with help from the observer only if necessary). This priority then forms the goal for a cycle of coaching with the teacher. During these coaching sessions, the teacher identifies and acts on their own solutions for improving their teaching.

SO WHAT'S THE IMPACT?

Well, like so many other schools, we find it difficult to fill all of our teaching vacancies without recruiting from abroad. Our overseas trained teachers are often young and newly qualified. Understandably, many of them are only able to manage a year away from family and friends in a totally alien country and culture. Consequently, we don't have much time to get them from 'inexperienced' to 'good.' The coaching approach has accelerated the learning process for all our new staff, and has led to the vast majority of them securing 'good' learning with their students as a minimum in a short space of time.

At Ashcroft, the number 7 is an important part of our coaching revolution!

In the module on giving feedback coach-style, Annie showed us how to identify the 7 key features of any area of the school that we wished to evaluate. It sounds so obvious and so easy, and yet…Try getting a group of staff to identify all the outstanding key features of an aspect of the school. Then challenge them to whittle the list down to an agreed, definitive shortlist of the 7 most important features.

The process is an invaluable professional development exercise within itself! It's a process we now use at Ashcroft with staff and students whenever we wish to define an area of provision and evaluate it. For example, staff and students used this process to agree the 7 key features of a positive learning climate in lessons.

LUTON'S COACHING REVOLUTION

I began this case study by confessing that I'm passionate about coaching. I now have to qualify that and confess that I'm passionate about Annie's coaching system. In fact, I'm positively evangelical about it, as my colleagues across Luton will testify.

My attitude is simple; if I've found a school-improvement system that works and has amazing and proven impact in so many different ways, why would I not share it with my colleagues who are working equally hard to improve their schools for the benefit of their children?

Thankfully, many of my colleagues in Luton have decided to benefit from Annie's revolutionary coaching system.

The Primary Headteachers in the **Luton First Teaching School Alliance** are keen to develop their skills in offering school-to-school support across and beyond Luton. They have all been trained by Annie in basic coaching skills and giving feedback coach-style, and several Primary Headteachers have gone on to become accredited coaches, alongside their leadership teams.

The Secondary Headteachers in the **Luton Futures Collaborative Partnership** are also working hard to create an effective model of school-to-school support. We have decided to adopt a coaching approach to this work, and the group is currently enjoying being trained by Annie as accredited coaches.

The coaching revolution is spreading across Luton, and I'm really excited because anything that benefits staff will benefit the children in our schools. And our children deserve the best.

AND FINALLY...

I've been a Headteacher for many years, with the heavy responsibility of spending public money wisely. I have never before been in a position to say this, but I'm going to say it now...

> If you can only spend your professional development budget on one thing, then invest it in starting your own coaching revolution in your school using Annie's system.

The learning is extremely cost-effective and represents excellent value for money (music to your business manager's ears!) It can be applied with staff, students, parents, and in one's personal life.

There is no sell-by date; the coaching system will keep producing amazing results in many years to come. The return on investment is ongoing and timeless. It's an investment that impacts positively on hearts and mindsets. It changes the language used by staff. It impacts positively on the culture of the school (the hardest thing to change). And it produces measurable improvements in the quality of provision and standards across the school.

I'll be eternally grateful to Annie for sharing her expertise and her revolutionary coaching system with us.

Long live the revolution!

Get instant access to my powerful '12-Step Model' and unique coaching courses at:

www.training.coachinginschools.com

If you would like me to personally work with you, please visit:

www.coachinginschools.com/get-in-touch

For the 360° Feedback School Improvement (SI)
& School Self-Evaluation (SSE) Diagnostic Tool, please go to:

www.360feedbackinschools.com